Preaching the Pastoral Epistles

PROCLAMATION:
Preaching the New Testament

Before the rise of historical criticism as the dominant mode of interpretation in the eighteenth century, biblical commentaries were written for the church with homiletical interests in mind. Since the Enlightenment, the critical commentary has largely excluded ecclesiastical and homiletical interests. In introducing the Meyer series in 1831, H. A. W. Meyer set the standard for subsequent commentaries, indicating that this commentary would exclude philosophical and ecclesiastical concerns and would concentrate on what the original authors meant in their own historical context.

This standard creates a challenge for preachers whose task is to bring a living word to listeners, most of whom do not come to church out of anti-quarian interests. Some commentaries have attempted to overcome the gap between the historical interests of the critical commentary and the homileti-cal concerns of the preacher by publishing parallel sections—one providing critical scholarship and the other offering guidance for preaching.

While biblical scholars specialize in a specific genre or book of scrip-ture, preachers are responsible for interpreting the entire canon over an extended time. As commentaries are increasingly complex, few preachers have the opportunity to mine the information and reflect an awareness of contemporary scholarship on each passage. Thus they face the challenge of merging the horizons between critical scholarship and a living word for the congregation.

In these volumes, scholar-preachers and preacher-scholars offer a guide for preachers, bringing the horizons of past and present together. The series is not a typical commentary, but a guide for preachers that offers the results of scholarship for the sake of preaching. Writers in this series will reflect an awareness of critical scholarship but will not focus on the details involved in a commentary. Rather, they will offer the fruits of critical scholarship reflected in explanations of sections of the biblical text. After a brief discussion of the major issues in a book—the central issues—each volume will be arranged by sections with an eye to what is useful for the sermon.

Authors in the Proclamation series will describe the major focus of each section, recognizing the place of the passage in the context of the book. Authors will look to the rhetorical impact of the text, asking "what does the text do?" Does it reassure the hearers? Does it lead them in worship and praise? Does it indict? Does it encourage? The Proclamation series will guide preachers in recognizing the essential rhetorical focus of the passage towards representing the impact of the text for today.

While preachers offer a living word for a specific situation, they also speak to larger cultural issues that face every congregation. Consequently, writers in this series may employ their knowledge of the ancient situation to suggest how the ancient word speaks across the centuries to parallel situations in our own time.

Accompanying the discussion writers may employ sermons, outlines, or other resources that further empower today's preachers in making the use of scholarship for the good of the church today.

Series Editors:

James W. Thompson is Scholar in Residence in the Graduate School of Theology at Abilene Christian University as well as the editor for Restoration Quarterly.

Jason A. Myers is Associate Professor of Biblical Studies at Greensboro College, Greensboro, NC.

Preaching
THE PASTORAL EPISTLES

℘

Robert W. Wall

CASCADE *Books* • Eugene, Oregon

PREACHING THE PASTORAL EPISTLES

Proclamation: Preaching the New Testament

Cascade Books
An Imprint of Wipf and Stock Publishers
199 W. 8th Ave., Suite 3
Eugene, OR 97401

www.wipfandstock.com

PAPERBACK ISBN: 978-1-6667-1042-7
HARDCOVER ISBN: 978-1-6667-1043-4
EBOOK ISBN: 978-1-6667-1044-1

Cataloguing-in-Publication data:

Names: Wall, Robert W. [author].

Title: Preaching the Pastoral Epistles / by Robert W. Wall.

Description: Eugene, OR: Cascade Books, 2024 | Series: Proclamation: Preaching the New Testament | Includes bibliographic references

Identifiers: ISBN 978-1-6667-1042-7 (paperback) | ISBN 978-1-6667-1043-4 (hardcover) | ISBN 978-1-6667-1044-1 (ebook)

Subjects: LCSH: Bible.—Pastoral Epistles—Commentaries. | Bible.—Timothy, 1st—Commentaries. | Bible.—Timothy, 2nd—Commentaries. | Bible.—Titus—Commentaries. | Preaching—Biblical teaching.

Classification: BS491.2 W35 2024 (paperback) | BS491.2 (ebook)

VERSION NUMBER 04/08/24

For Tony Robinson,
friend and mentor

CONTENTS

2 Timothy

Titus

ACKNOWLEDGMENT

THIS IS A COMMENTARY for pastors. I am reminded that Paul's list of Spirit-appointed leaders to "equip the saints for their work of ministry" (Eph 4:11–12) includes a final pair of words often conjoined: "pastors and teachers." My sense is that this pairing is purposeful and right but that it can be placed together in ways that emphasize "teaching pastors" or "pastoring teachers." This is a commentary written for both kinds of spiritual leaders: those gifted and called as "teaching pastors" of congregations of Jesus-followers and those as "pastoring teachers" of classrooms of attentive students.

I want to acknowledge that this is a commentary that depends upon, even if its updates, work done a decade ago in preparing my two previous books on the Pauline Pastorals, the first for the Two Horizons New Testament Commentary, *1 &2 Timothy and Titus*, and a second, also published by Eerdmans, that features a dialogue between myself and my friend Tony Robinson, *Called to Lead: Paul's Letters to Timothy for a New Day*. I've included both in this book's bibliography. The translations of each letter are my own.

The publication of this new book, especially for the Proclamation Commentary series, provides me an opportunity to pay modest tribute to my deeply affecting friendship of many years with Tony R. I know of no other clergyperson who better embodies the role and work of the "teaching pastor" than Tony Robinson. May God raise up, call, and gift others to copy Tony's Spirit-led example in equipping Christ's church for the ministry of God's gospel in today's world.

Rob Wall
Pentecost 2023

INTRODUCING THE
PASTORAL EPISTLES

SINCE THE SECOND CENTURY, 1–2 Timothy and Titus have been read together to help order a Christian congregation's life and mission. While the title "Pastoral Epistles" (PE) was an invention of early modern criticism as the commonsense impression of the contents of this subcollection of Pauline letters, it squares with the earliest reference to their purpose in the "Muratorian Fragment" (170–210 CE) to "bring order to ecclesiastical discipline." On close reading, the practical instructions and moral injunctions that characterize these three letters target the instruction of two spiritual leaders of earliest Christianity mentioned in Acts, namely Timothy and Titus, to whom they are addressed. All are written in the literary genre of *paraenesis*, compositions consisting of moral exhortations and practical instructions arranged topically to guide the professional and personal formation of a community's leaders. All three are also letters of succession in which the sender, in this case the apostle Paul, prepares his handpicked successors, Timothy and Titus, for their future ministry in his absence.

While all three are attributed to Paul, modern scholars since Schleiermacher have noted both their agreements and differences with other Pauline letters in vocabulary, pastoral tone, ecclesial structure, ethical rules (*paraenesis*), and theological substance. Additionally, the letters' profile of a canonical Paul whose apostleship is of singular importance for God's plan of salvation (cf. 1 Tim 2:7; 2 Tim 2:1–2; Titus 1:2–3) suggests a later, idealized reception of memories of Paul's apostolic persona and theological grammar preserved by members of his inner circle and put in circulation (perhaps with other Pauline letters) following his death. On this basis, most scholars today conclude that the historical Paul probably did not write 1 Timothy and perhaps not even Titus or 2 Timothy. While this consensus remains contested among scholars—I personally find, for example, historical criticism's arguments against Pauline authorship unpersuasive—its unfortunate effect within the church and its academy has been to neglect them: they are rarely studied in seminary or preached in the church, even when the lectionary calls for it as a "second reading."

The deep logic that silences the PE operates at two levels: at an epistemic level, if the real Paul did not write them then they lack credible authority in forming the one holy catholic and *apostolic* church. At a more practical level, apart from the array of famous one-liners that have become the staple of catechism classes for centuries, mention is made of their so-called "texts of terror" that have been used or abused to push sisters and brothers to the harsh margins of a community called to instantiate God's love in the world. First Timothy 2:11–14 is such a text, especially when received with its history of patriarchal interpretation that has denied God's call of gifted women to Christian ministry or has restricted them to domestic chores. In a similar way, the catalog of credentials for church leadership given in 1 Timothy 3, even though presented as a guideline, has been prescribed in an artless manner to exclude mature believers from using their talents to secure the congregation's spiritual and social well-being. And the sentiment that the role of slaves is to benefit their masters (1 Tim 6:1–2), even when contextualized by the social world of ancient Roman culture, sounds a discordant note in today's world, which has been put on alert by the horrors of human trafficking. No wonder many modern Christians, who, like the author of these letters, seek to adapt the gospel to culturally acceptable patterns of behavior, find these instructions offensive.

Within more conservative Protestant communions, where the grammar of faith is ordered by the Reformation's theology of *sola scriptura*, the situation is different but no less tortured. The PE are approved reading and practiced but not until considerable effort is expended to protect them from modern criticism as genuinely Pauline, divinely inspired, and authoritative. Even though accepted as such, their instruction is typically applied only selectively to defend a congregation's countervailing orthodoxy or social practices against liberal religion, which is thought to have advanced women clergy too quickly or to have been too soft on perceived heresy and modernity's moral relativism.

In any case, I would suggest that whether or not the PE are practiced in the worship and instruction of a Christian congregation is less the result of a verdict about their authorship or how they square with current social norms and more the result of a congregation's ecclesiology of scripture. The neglect of any writing canonized by and for the formation of God's people results from a failure to affirm and privilege scripture as the essential medium of God's self-presentation to God's people. Church is the primary residence of scripture; church is where people hear God's word proclaimed and practiced and church is where God is learned and a deepened love for God is cultivated by the hearing of God's word. Second, a congregation's neglect of the PE instantiates a failure to recognize that *the Spirit-led church* is the real author of its two-testament Bible: the church formed the Bible in the fullness of time in order to form the church throughout time. This commentary is a performance of my belief that God's Spirit has sanctified and continues to inspire the PE to lead Jesus' followers into the truth about God's providential way of ordering the world.

Ironically, even though the PE were probably first used and then canonized to help train the spiritual leaders of earliest Christianity, they are rarely taught to do the same in most seminaries today. The trickle-down result of modern criticism's silencing of these letters is that they are rarely preached or taught in local parishes. This commentary is written in large part to help pastors and teachers restore the proper role imagined for this subcollection of Pauline letters in the origins of the church's scripture. The following five questions help pour the foundation for this holy end. The responses I give to them are contested among thoughtful and faithful Bible scholars; they are given to orient readers of this commentary but also to invite them into a conversation about scripture's authority that is often messy and never easy.

1. Did the real Paul write the PE? Our conversation about the PE will name "Paul" as their author and "Timothy" and "Titus" as the recipients of his correspondence. While these attributions are not secured by historical analysis, since the hard evidence necessary to do so is much too sparse and uncertain to validate such a claim with confidence, they are secured by the church's recognition of them as Pauline. They should be read and used as an integral part of the canonical collection of Pauline letters, which is based on recognition of their theological perspicuity and their usefulness in the formation of God's people in doing every good work of God (so 2 Tim 3:17). Virtually every modern commentary on the PE begins with something of a defense of their uncertain authorship. There are two reasons why this work is thought necessary. First, scholars often equate a book's authorship with its enduring authority as scripture. This may seem like a surprising formula since most of the church's two-testament Bible consists of anonymous compositions, written under the name of a prophet or an apostle to locate them in a long tradition of eyewitnesses to God's presence and activity in the history of God's people.

Second, especially letters gathered together in the Pauline canonical collection claim a theological coherence based upon their single authorship. That is, if the real Paul did not write the PE, not only is their per se theological content and usefulness for theological understanding suspect but they cannot be used in forming scripture's Pauline witness to the gospel. In any case, the real referent of scripture is *God*; the "what about God" or even the theological "why" of a text has proven vastly more important in the history of a text's interpretation in and for the church (less so in the academy) than the identity of the one who wrote it. The academy's rejection of the PE as genuinely Pauline or "apostolic" on historical grounds is based on what Andrew Lincoln has called an "authorial fallacy" (Lincoln, *Ephesians*, lxxii–lxxiii). According to this fallacy, the criterion of a text's apostolicity is based on whether or not modern historical reconstructions "prove" a real apostle had a hand in the production of the text. A critical orthodoxy based on the "assured results" of leading scholars on this point often predetermines a judgment about a text's usefulness or continuing authority. In fact, Luke Timothy Johnson names the modern assumption that Paul did not write these letters an *idola theatri* ("a theatrical idol"), after Sir Francis Bacon's rejection of the unquestioned acceptance of any academic dogma. The PE are marginalized in the study of Pauline letters in most seminaries and so also in the preaching ministry of clergy because most scholars accept the verdict of critical orthodoxy regarding their authorship without careful examination.

This Proclamation Commentary grants priority to the church's claim that these are Pauline letters. Its emphasis remains on the text rather than on who wrote it because this is where the church has placed its emphasis in Christian worship and instruction. But in doing so, I recognize the inherent elasticity of words used over time and the multiple possible functions of their grammatical relations. Further changes in the perception of a text's meaning may result from new evidence and different exegetical strategies and from interpreters who sort out a text's natural ambiguity within diverse social and theological locations. In fact, the sort of neutrality toward biblical texts that modern criticism applauds is now held with deep suspicion because our ordinary experience with texts of all kinds teaches us that textual meaning cannot be considered absolute for all time, whether as the assured conclusion of the scholarly guild (which is constantly adjusting its assured claims!) or as some meaning determined by (and known only to) God at the time of a text's composition. Thus, the fluid nature of exegesis resists the old dichotomy between past and present meanings, and between authorial and canonical intentions.

2. Why include *the PE* among Paul's *thirteen* canonical letters? Perhaps the logical next question is to ask why *did* the church receive and include these letters in its final edition of the NT. The "canonical approach" to biblical interpretation followed in this commentary shifts a reader's focus from the moment of composition when Paul wrote the PE to Timothy and Titus to a later historical moment sometime toward the end of the second century when the church added the PE to a ten-letter Pauline collection then in wide circulation and use to complete its now thirteen-letter Pauline canon. Such an interest is deeply rooted in a belief that God's Spirit guides the church's choices in forming its biblical canon; after all, the church is a community in which the Spirit dwells and works (Eph 2:21–22). In this sense, when we speak of scripture as a "canon" of holy texts or its practices within the church as "canonical," we do so in affirmation that the inspiring presence of God's Spirit is at work among and within scripture's faithful readers no matter their time zone, using these precious texts in drawing them into a more intimate and wakeful fellowship with the living God.

The church's formation of its two-testament Bible creates a literary aesthetic that is substantively and functionally different from those critical collections scholars compose according to their historical critical conclusions about authorship, date, genre, and the social location of a group of biblical writings. The seven-letter Pauline canon (without the PE, and typically Ephesians, Colossians, 2 Thessalonians) accepted and used by many Pauline scholars to guide their quest for the historical Paul differs in shape and substance from the thirteen-letter Pauline corpus (with the PE) that was fashioned and fixed during the church's canonical process. Even though the canonical approach should not be considered a substitute for critical reconstructions (or deconstructions) of the Pauline letter collection, it places a premium on reading any Pauline letter within its canonical rather than historical context. At the very moment when the three PE were added to the extant ten-letter Pauline collection (toward the end of the second century), the church recognized that it had reached its final (or "canonical") form—a literary form that upon its use in an array of settings is found most effective in shaping a Christian congregation's understanding of scripture's Pauline witness.

Think of the canonical process as a type of evolutionary mechanism. New external threats present or on the horizon by the mid-second century, a change of audiences, along with new responsibilities that come on line to meet the internal pressures of an expanding religious movement all forge a different ecclesial environment from that of Paul's original mission. Consequently, a collection of his letters needed to be adapted in order for his apostolate to survive into the next generation or within another cultural setting of an ever-expanding mission. Put positively, subsequent readers of Paul, about the time the Pauline canon reached its final canonical form—such as Irenaeus and especially Tertullian—found the sweep of its concerns readily adaptable to this new environment. In my estimation, the addition of the Pastorals to complete the Pauline canon made it so. My affirmation is that the church's preservation, canonization, and continuing use of the thirteen Pauline letters in their final form, whether in its preaching or catechesis, is predicated on its adaptability to the social and religious exigencies facing the one holy catholic and apostolic church today.

In this sense, we contend that the final literary form of scripture is a work of aesthetic excellence. That is, the overall literary form of the church's two-testament Bible, the order of its various collections, and even the order of books within these canonical collections is purposeful of an orderly way of reading scripture. The NT is not read before or without the OT; the fourfold Gospel story of Jesus is foundational of every other collection that follows. Paul is not read without Jesus or the book of Acts, nor is Hebrews or the Catholic Epistles collection read without first reading Paul. And the entire Bible concludes with a reading of the Apocalypse of John. Through its orderly and Spirit-inspired performances of scripture in worship, catechesis, mission, and personal devotion, the church is empowered to form a holy people who know and love God.

The critical footnote to this brief overview of canonization is that the PE were finally folded into an incomplete collection of Pauline letters to complete it based on a résumé of ecclesial performances that demonstrated not only their usefulness in "bringing order to ecclesiastical discipline" but also in helping make better sense of the Pauline witness as a whole. In this sense, the church's decisions were rational but based on evidence of their inspired utility in "ordering ecclesiastical discipline" and not their inspired authorship. The enduring excellence of the PE is best evinced when they continue to be preached and taught for this same holy end.[1]

3. Why were the PE written? Commentaries sometimes introduce the PE by plotting an unwritten (and unknown) narrative of the events that occasioned their composition. Most tell the story of Christian teachers who oppose Pauline orthodoxy, and thus the instructions and exhortations of each letter are interpreted as mirrored responses to a range of intramural conflicts that unsettled earliest Pauline Christianity. In fact, however, while Paul mentions opponents and sometimes even names them, he does so only in passing. Their mention can hardly explain what occasioned Paul to write the PE. The profile of Paul's opponents is too thinly drawn and rarely is mention made of what they taught; most instructions are practical in kind and directed at congregational or personal practices that have little to do with the presence or teaching of opponents.

More simply, the character of these letters is better understood by their salutation, which mentions Paul's departure (cf. 1 Tim 1:3; Titus 1:5) and implies thereby the absence of his apostolic persona and authority (cf. 1 Tim 2:7; Titus 1:3) in pagan Ephesus, where a fledging Christian congregation is being formed under the leadership of a newly appointed and still unproven leader, Timothy. By analogy, then, the variegated instructions, theological formulae, and pastoral admonitions found in both letters are apropos of a succession of new leaders who must struggle to get their religious bearings afresh in the absence of their charismatic and experienced leader. Indeed, false teachers, immature believers, incompetent or unprepared leaders, uncertain organization, disorderly relationships with others inside and outside the congregation all pose real threats to apostolic succession when Paul is no longer the go-to person when dealing with a congregation's needs. It's up to the next in line, with only Paul's instructions as a guide.

Reading 1 and 2 Timothy may well help construct what Charles Taylor has called a "social imaginary" of how an apostolic succession challenges a variety of social and political relationships at ground level.[2] Paul's instructions to Timothy, since canonized for the church catholic of every age, define a set of normative practices and beliefs, both congregational and individual, that help every new batch of congregational leaders reimagine how they should follow Paul's apostolic lead but in an ever-changing post-apostolic

---

1. Wall, *1 & 2 Timothy and Titus*, 15–27.
2. Cf. Taylor, *A Secular Age*.

setting. Simply put, these letters help readers imagine what Paul might do were he here among us today. Their force is less prescriptive than intuitive of how a sacred household should be organized, why it should be organized in this way (practically and theologically), and also what anticipates the material effects of doing so. Indeed, the earliest canon list (Muratorian, ca. 200), which includes the Pastorals among Paul's canonical letters, claims their not insignificant role is to provide "ecclesiastical discipline"; we suggest this is chief among their ongoing performances as scripture.

4. How does the literary form of the PE convey a word about God? Since the genre of sacred literature carries theological freight, it is an important element of preaching scripture as God's word for God's people. In this regard, whatever occasions a letter also helps to determine the form of written response. Letters of succession, such as the PE, are *paraenetic*: they are written to instruct and exhort, to provide examples and models to imitate (cf. Acts 20:17–35). But in doing so, they also target a particular crisis occasioned by any succession of leaders, made even more critical in this case because the leader is an apostle who is providentially given a word from God for this moment of salvation's history (see comment on Titus 1:1–3). This is an apostolic succession; and its sacred deposit must be safeguarded for the next generation (cf. 2 Tim 1:13–14; 2:1–2). Significantly, this kind of letter also facilitates the role the PE perform within the Pauline canon.

Of course, person-to-person letters like the PE took many forms in the ancient world. Most were written communication to bridge the distance between two persons. Oratory was an important social convention of Paul's world, and letters were the literary expression of speech. Among the various kinds of letters preserved from the ancient world, perhaps the most common is private correspondence, similar in function and form to the PE. We now possess literally thousands of ancient papyrus letters, stored in museums around the world, which reflect a variety of transactions even though following a standard literary pattern: an opening greeting, the main body, and a concluding benediction.

Letters of antiquity began with formal greetings so that the recipient would know the sender immediately upon unrolling the scroll. Paul's letters generally followed this well-known script: "Sender to recipient, greetings." In personal letters such as these, this formula was amplified to highlight the nature of the personal relationship between sender and recipient; this in turn clarified the expected response of the letter's recipient to its instructions. In the case of his correspondence to these friends to whom he delegates his apostolic authority, Paul's address not only emphasizes a personal relationship of long standing, but also his spiritual authority toward them. Especially when the New Testament reader has the Paul of Acts in mind, Paul's identification of himself as an "apostle of Christ Jesus" posits the religious importance of his mission and message for the future of the church, which Timothy has been delegated to organize in Ephesus.

The main body of a personal letter takes up the business at hand. (In this sense, it functions much like a sermon does in a worship service.) Differences of emphasis and vocabulary that the careful reader notes from Pauline letter to letter reflect the range of controversies and crises that Paul considers and seeks to resolve in the main body of his various letters. He gives advice, renders instruction, makes commands, corrects doctrine, rebukes false teachers—all according to his understanding of scripture's roles within the faith community (cf. 2 Tim 3:16b). The purpose of the main body of a personal letter follows this strategy but ostensibly with a particular person rather than congregation in view. The subject matter of 1 Timothy and Titus is primarily concerned with conveying instructions that would order congregational life in pagan places—not unlike the early second-century Didache and other Christian writings across the next several centuries for an expanding missionary church. The main body of 2 Timothy is quite different, with a heightened sense of Paul's passing and the importance of Timothy's role to carry on his legacy to the next generation—a kind of literary "last will and testament" of the revered apostle.

The concluding words of a Pauline letter, including these, include many elements. While always a benedictory blessing of some kind is found, miscellaneous greetings, exhortations, itinerary, summaries of concern, and other personal reminders are included as well. What this suggests about these letters is that they were not intended by Paul as "private" letters but for a wider readership beyond Timothy. Of the various functions performed by private letters, all three of the PE are letters of "instruction and order," though the instructions contained in 1 Timothy and Titus intend to order a congregation's life with God and one another, while those given in 2 Timothy are more personal and seek to order Timothy's life after the model exemplified and instructed by Paul. The more personal tone and themes of 2 Timothy suggest a professional relationship between a mentor and apprentice that seems to require equal measure of encouragement with a firm reminder of the important mission at hand. This observation is important

9

for understanding the literary genre of the PE as different kinds of paraenesis or letters of instruction that advise the recipient how to order relationships and solve problems. First Timothy and Titus are written in the genre of *mandata principis* ("mandates" from the "principal" of the pack)—official letters from a superior to an administrative associate for use at a specific location.[3] Similarly, Johnson observes that 2 Timothy is also paraenesis but is most like the advice given in a "last will and testament"; however, in my terms, 2 Timothy reads more like a "succession letter" to order a change in a community's leadership. These literary observations not only explain the occasion of the PE but also their continuing role for a church that does its work in the absence of the apostle and is charged, as Timothy was, to safeguard the Pauline apostolate for the next generation.

This commentary will introduce and work through each of the three letters in turn. They were individually designed and written by Paul and individually occasioned by the circumstances facing Timothy and Titus. Nonetheless, I will keep at the forefront the original intention of the church in canonizing all three as a subcollection of Pauline letters. They always appear together in the early canon lists and compilations of scripture or not at all; they should be read together today and always in conversation with other Pauline letters.

5. How can we use personal letters written to individuals to form the theological understanding and Christian life of a congregation? The preceding Q&A raises a very important question for those preparing to preach these texts to a congregation or teach them to a classroom of students from different faith traditions. The diverse and abrupt character of paraenetic literature such as Paul's Timothy correspondence makes it difficult for the reader to follow the flow: there is no plotline, no clear rhetorical design that enables the reader to track easily the argument made. But there is an overarching flowchart that is followed so that the discrete bits of paraenesis are linked together by repeated words that help readers cobble together a vision for life and work. Familiar materials are used to help craft such a vision that is easily accessible to the reader.

In this case, Paul uses familiar topoi, much like he does when cataloguing cardinal virtues to habituate or commonsense vices to avoid. Stories of the good soldier, disciplined athlete, and hardworking farmer are used even today to illustrate our moral instruction. Their use in canonical texts is routine, since their ambiguity allows for more flexibility

3. Johnson, *The First and Second Letters to Timothy*, 97.

when applying the gospel truth to faithful practice. This same literary characteristic, however, sometimes makes it difficult for the reader to understand the particular motive and plain sense of what is written. In the case of this passage, the topoi of hard workers shape an impression of why the faithful tradent must share in the suffering of the Lord's apostle. The importance of hard work is characteristic of faithfulness and a familiar feature of Pauline exhortation (cf. Col 4:13).

In general terms, we might ask: What relevance does a personal letter written in the genre of paraenesis to an individual about the particular problems facing that person a couple of millennia ago have for today's congregations and classrooms populated by many diverse individuals? On the one hand, I maintain that the most effective use of the PE is to train congregational leaders, whether clergy or laity, who in turn lead by nurturing their worshiping communities in God's direction. These are letters best used as part of a seminary's biblical curriculum to instruct and prepare prospective clergy for parish ministry. On the other hand, lessons from the PE are consistently found in the Common Lectionary, indicating their role in proclaiming scripture as God's word for God's people. The universalizing effect of canonizing the PE transforms our approach to their interpretation. Of course, we know that while the church catholic, West and East, receives a stable or timeless canon of biblical texts, it does not receive a stable and timeless canonical interpretation of those texts. The church does not have a Talmud to read with our Torah. In fact, if one were to track, for example, the two-thousand-year history of interpreting any single passage of the PE, they would quickly discover how variegated is their *interpretation* and use in worship and instruction.

When preachers adapt biblical passages to their congregation's worlds—to the things that occasion a hearing of God's word at any moment in time or place—they must engage in acts of analogical imagination. Instead of individuals asked to continue in the tradition of the apostle Paul, they must now reimagine how a passage can guide an entire congregation to continue in this same apostolic tradition. Instead of the ancient "strange worlds" of Timothy's Ephesus or Titus's Crete, preachers must now reimagine how Paul's instructions to his young protegees can be adapted to a contemporary world of today's Christian congregations. The purpose of this commentary is to help clergy and teachers do this hard but holy work.

In fact, the holy end of preaching scripture is catechesis: the initiation of a community of believers into a deeper understanding of God and of

God's way of salvation. Such knowledge not only inspires greater love of God and our neighbor but cultivates a fully informed intellect—a mind that loves God—that enables the instruction of others but also makes the instructed more wakeful of those falsehoods, sometimes clothed in Christian rhetoric, that lead believers away from God. The "sermon sketches" that accompany my brief "exegetical reflections" on the ten selected passages from the PE are purposeful of a congregation's catechesis: instruction that is a word on target in the formation of a congregation that knows what it means to be God's people and to do what God's people are called to do.

6. Should we read the PE as three individual letters written at different times to different individuals about different settings and circumstances; or do we read these three letters as a threefold whole? This is one of several ambivalences that characterize the modern study of these Pauline letters. Both approaches have merit and the preacher or teacher may find that both are beneficial and will seek to integrate them when preaching or teaching them to a congregation or class. Following modern criticism's interest in studying texts at the moment of their composition, I have provided brief introductions to each individual letter that seeks to clarify the occasion, the genre, the interests of each letter, with the presumption that each letter will be preached or taught as a separate unit of instruction from the other two. If one were to do so, however, in a manner consistent with modern criticism, then the chronological order might be preferred as well. One would thus begins with the earliest letter written—most think Titus—and then the next written—most think 2 Timothy—and then conclude with 1 Timothy. A subtext of such a series of sermons or lessons would seek to capture the evolving content of Paul's self-understanding and witness to God's way of salvation.

If however one were to follow the church's post-biblical interests in "ecclesiastical discipline" (see above)—a century after their composition, at the moment of the church's recognition of their enduring authority and consequent inclusion in canonical collection of Pauline letters—then not only would the current order of the PE be maintained but they would also be studied and preached together as a threefold whole. I have not prepared this Proclamation Commentary to follow this canonical track but have hinted at it often in my exegetical notes. For those interested in this approach into the PE, I would encourage you to consider finding ways to preach or teach the three letters together as a mutually informing whole as you prepare your sermons or lessons. Perhaps a thematic approach that integrates the teaching of all three letters into a common "pastoral theology for the church"; or a set of dialogues between the Paul of 1 Timothy and 2 Timothy or Titus. The prospect of reading the PE from front to back or back to front and comparing the two sequences for the benefit of a congregation's catechesis makes for an interesting sermon series!

1 TIMOTHY

A Snapshot of 1 Timothy

1 Timothy begins with a potential problem that prompts its production: Paul has departed for Macedonia and has delegated his important Ephesian mission to a young associate, Timothy (1:3). To make this succession from charismatic apostle to inexperienced pastor as smooth as possible, 1 Timothy combines pastoral instruction, personal exhortation, and pointed theological summaries that intends to guide the continuity of an apostolic tradition in absence of its pioneer (cf. 6:20).

Noted throughout the letter are various threats to the ministry of the gospel—bad theology, ineffective pedagogy, opposing teachers, imprudent social manners, unqualified leadership, sloppy ecclesial practices, distracted discipleship—all of which might undermine the forward movement of the Pauline mission once he (with his apostolic gifts) departs Ephesus for Macedonia. In this sense, Paul's instructions and exhortations to Timothy are constructive and practical, not polemical. This is a letter occasioned by Paul's absence and not by the presence of false teachers in Ephesus.

For this reason, the centerpiece of this letter is the aggregate of Paul's wisdom for a young and inexperienced pastor (1:18–20; 3:14–16; 4:7–16; 6:11–16). For all his handwringing over possible problems, Paul's principal concern is Timothy, that his calling and the "spiritual gifts" given to him are faithfully practiced in forming a covenant-keeping "household of God" (3:14–16). The expansive range of topics covered in this letter intend to order social relationships within the congregation's membership and to locate this well-ordered congregation as a witness to God in an increasingly hostile world. Timothy's ordination is to teach and embody these instructions "because by doing so you will save both yourself and those who listen to you" (4:16).

Finally, within its canonical context, the theological and ethical summaries found throughout 1 Timothy (1:11–17; 2:3–7; 3:16; 4:4; 6:7–10, 11–12, 15–16) are apt distillations of the Pauline theology found in his other letters (cf. Rom 1:16–17). They bring into focus his grammar of faith and provide a framework for reading his entire canonical collection as Christian scripture.

Paul Greets Timothy

1:1 From Paul an apostle of Christ Jesus by the command of God our Savior and Christ Jesus our hope, 2 to Timothy, genuine son in faith: grace, mercy, and peace from God the Father and Christ Jesus our Lord.

A Congregation's Catechism

3 As I requested you to do when leaving for Macedonia: stay longer in Ephesus so that you may instruct certain individuals not to teach heretical teachings, 4 nor pay attention to myths and unending family trees. Their teaching only encourages idle speculation rather than faithfulness to God's economy of the real world. 5 The aim of our instruction is loving relationships that come from a pure heart, good conscience, and sincere faith. 6 Some have rejected this and have turned to fruitless discussion, 7 wanting to be Torah teachers without understanding either what they are saying or what they are claiming. 8 We know, for example, that the law is good if used

lawfully. [9] We understand a law is not for an innocent person but for the lawless and rebellious, godless and sinners, unholy and profane, for those who commit patricide and matricide, for murderers, [10] the sexually unfaithful, sexual deviants, slave dealers, liars, perjurers, and anyone else who acts contrary to healthy teaching, [11] which agrees with the glorious gospel of the blessed God that has been entrusted to me.

[12] I thank Christ Jesus our Lord who has strengthened me and considered me faithful, appointing me to a ministry [13] even though I was an ex-blasphemer and persecutor, a violent man who was shown mercy because I acted in ignorance and unbelief. [14] Our Lord's grace poured all over me along with the faith and love that are in Christ Jesus. [15] This teaching is a core belief worthy of unqualified acceptance: "Christ Jesus came into the world to save sinners"—among whom I am first! [16] But I was shown mercy for this reason, that Christ Jesus might thoroughly demonstrate patience first in me as the role model for those who come to believe in him for eternal life. [17] Now to the eternal King, to the immortal, invisible, and only God, be honor and glory forever and ever. Amen.

Shipwrecked Faith

[18] Timothy my son, I entrust this instruction to you according to the prophecies once made about you so that you may fight the good fight with those [19] who have faith and good conscience. Some have subverted and have shipwrecked their faith. [20] Among them are Hymenaeus and Alexander, whom I have handed over to Satan so that they may learn not to blaspheme.

A Congregation's Worship Practices

2:1 First of all, therefore, I request that supplications, prayers, petitions, thanksgivings be offered for everybody—[2] even the kings and all those in positions of authority—so that we may lead a peaceful and calm life in full godliness and holiness. [3] This is good and acceptable in the eyes of God our Savior, [4] who desires to save everybody and for them to come to a knowledge of the truth: [5] There is one God and one mediator between God and humankind, a man, Christ Jesus, [6] who gave himself a ransom for everybody, the witness at the right time. [7] I have been appointed its herald, an apostle—I speak the truth and do not lie—and a teacher of the nations in matters of faith and truth.

[8] Therefore, I want men to pray in every place with their holy hands lifted up without anger or argument. [9] Likewise, women should adorn themselves modestly and prudently with sensible attire, without braided hair, gold, pearls, or costly clothes, [10] but rather with good works suitable for pious women. [11] Let a woman learn attentively in full submission. [12] I do not allow a woman to teach or to have authority over a man but to be a quiet student. [13] For Adam was formed first, then Eve, [14] and Adam was not deceived, rather the woman was deceived and became a sinner; [15] she will be saved, however, through childbearing (if they continue in faith and love and holiness with prudence. 3:1a This teaching is a core belief).

The Character and Cast of Congregational Leadership

3:1b Someone who aspires to become an administrator desires a good work. [2] Therefore the administrator must be blameless: the husband of one wife, clearheaded, modest, respectable, hospitable, a skilled teacher, [3] not a drunk or a bully but gentle, peaceable, generous. [4] He must manage his own household well, holding children in submission with complete respect—[5] for if someone does not know how to manage his own household, how can he care for God's church? [6] He must not be newly converted so not to be arrogant and slip into the devil's condemnation. [7] He must have good references from outsiders so not to slip into disgrace, the devil's trap.

[8] Likewise, servants must be honorable, so not duplicitous, nor a drunk or greedy. [9] They should hold to the mystery of the faith with a clear conscience; [10] let those who serve first be tested and found blameless. [11] Likewise, women must be proper, not slanderous, prudent, faithful in all things. [12] Let

the servants be the husband of one wife who manage children and their own household well; [13] for those who serve well acquire for themselves a good position and much confidence within the faith that is in Christ Jesus.

[14] While I hope to come soon to you, I write these instructions to you [15] so that if I am delayed you will know how you must behave as the pillar and foundation of the truth within the household of God, which is the church of the living God. [16] Indeed, the mystery of holy living we confess is important:

> He was revealed in flesh and confirmed by Spirit
>
> seen by angels and proclaimed among the nations
>
> believed worldwide and exalted in glory.

4:1 But in fact the Spirit says that in the latter times some will abandon the faith, adhering to deceptive spirits and doctrines of demons [2] because of the hypocrisy of deceptive liars and cauterized consciences. [3] For example, they forbid marriage and eating foods that God has created to be received with thanksgiving by those who believe and know the truth. [4] For everything God created is good and nothing received with thanksgiving is rejected [5] since these things are sanctified by God's word and prayer. [6] If you instruct these things to believers you will be a good servant of Christ Jesus, apprenticed according to the teachings of the faith, the good doctrine, you have followed. [7a] Have nothing to do with profane and silly myths.

Practice These Things

[7b] Train yourself for godliness. [8] While physical training has some value, a holy life has value for everything, holding promise for both this life and the life to come. [9-10] This teaching is a core belief and worthy of unqualified acceptance for it is the aim of our work and struggle: "Our hope is set on the living God who is the Savior of all people, especially those who believe." [11] Command compliance to these instructions and teach. [12] Let no one despise your youth, but until I arrive set a pattern

for believers in speech, in public conduct, in love, in faith, in purity. [13] Pay attention to public reading, preaching, and teaching. [14] Do not neglect the spiritual gift in you, which was given to you through prophecy with the laying on of hands by the council of elders. [15] Practice these things; live by them so that your progress may be observed by all. [16] Pay close attention to yourself and to your teaching; for by doing this you will save both yourself and those who listen to you.

Bringing Order to the House

5:1 Do not rebuke an older man harshly. Encourage him as though he were your father, younger men as though brothers, [2] older women as though mothers, and younger women as though sisters with complete purity.

[3] Care for widows who are truly needy. [[4] But if a particular widow has children or a relative, they should first learn to practice their piety by taking care of their own household and so repay their parents; for this pleases God.] [5] If truly needy and completely on her own, the widow puts her hope in God and pleas and prays continually night and day. [6] But the one who lives extravagantly dies even though alive. [7] Instruct these things so that they will be blameless. [8] Especially if someone does not care for a member of their household, he repudiates the faith and is worse than an unbeliever.

[9] Make a list of widows older than sixty, the wife of one man, [10] a reputation for good works—she has raised children, practiced hospitality, washed the feet of believers, helped those during difficult times, accompanied by all kinds of good works. [11] But decline younger widows, for when they are distracted from Christ and choose to marry, [12] judgment results because they invalidate the prior confession of faith. [13] Moreover, by going from house to house they learn laziness, and not only laziness but how to gossip and meddle, saying things they shouldn't. [14] Therefore, I prefer that younger widows marry, raise children, keep house, to give the opponent no opportunity to slander us; [15] for some have already turned away to follow Satan. [16] If any female believer has widows, she

should care for them and not burden the church in order that it can help other widows who are truly needy.

[17] Request a double honorarium for elderly men who lead well, especially those who labor in public speaking and teaching. [18] For the Scripture says, "Do not muzzle the ox that is threshing" and "The worker is worthy of his wages." [19] Do not respond to an accusation leveled against an elder if not confirmed "by two or three witnesses." [20] Discipline those who sin before the entire congregation in order to provoke fear in those present. [21] Bring testimony before God, Christ Jesus, and the elect angels in order that you will discharge these instructions without prejudice and without making a biased claim. [22a] Do not ordain anyone hastily.

[22b] Do not share in the sins of others. Keep yourself pure. [23] Stop drinking just water but use a little wine for your upset stomach and frequent illnesses! [24] The sins of some folks are blatant, leading to judgment, whilst others follow close behind; [25] on the other hand, the good works of still others are evident and cannot remain hidden from view.

6:1 Those who carry the yoke of slavery must respect their own masters as deserving every honor so that the name of God and the Teaching may not be reviled. [2a] Those who have believers as masters must not despise them because they are brothers; rather, they must serve them more faithfully since the recipients of good work are beloved believers.

Money Problems and Possibilities

6:2b Teach and encourage these things: [3] If someone teaches differently and does not come to agree with the healthy teachings about our Lord Jesus Christ—teaching that accords with godliness—[4] he is arrogant, understands nothing, but has an unhealthy interest in contesting the meaning of words that provoke envy, dissension, slander, evil suspicion [5] and persistent argument among those who are corrupt and deprived of the truth, who think that piety is profitable. [6] Indeed, there is great profit when piety is combined with self-sufficiency! [7] For we brought nothing into the world and so are able to take nothing out: [8] we shall be satisfied with food and shelter.

[9] Those who are determined to be rich, however, are tripped up into temptation and a trap—many foolish and harmful cravings—that plunge them headlong into ruin and destruction. [10] For the love of money is the root of all kinds of evil. Some who have aspired for wealth have wandered from the faith and have impaled themselves with many pains.

[11] But you, o man of God, flee from all this! Instead, pursue moral rectitude, piety, faith, love, endurance, gentleness. [12] Compete the good race of the faith! Lay hold of eternal life for which you were called and have confessed the good confession before many witnesses! [13] I exhort you before God who dispenses life to all things and before Christ Jesus who made the good confession when testifying before Pontius Pilate. [14] Obey this command without fault or failure until the appearing of our Lord Jesus Christ, [15] whose timing God alone determines—God, the blessed and only Ruler, King of the kings and Lord of the lords, [16] who alone has immortality, dwells in unapproachable light, whom no human has seen or is able to see, to whom is honor and everlasting sovereignty. Amen.

[17] To the rich of the present age: tell them not to be arrogant, or to count on the uncertainty of riches but on God who richly offers us all things for our enjoyment; [18] to do good—to be rich in good deeds—and to be generous communicants, [19] storing up for themselves a good foundation for the future in order to lay hold of what is truly life.

Guard the Tradition

[20] O Timothy, stand guard over the tradition. Avoid worldly chitchat and fictions of the so-called "knowledge." [21] By claiming it, some have missed the target concerning the faith. Grace be with you all.

Chapter 1

A CONGREGATION'S CATECHISM

Exegetical Notes on 1 Timothy 1

PAUL'S DEPARTURE FROM EPHESUS requires that Timothy stay behind to lead the Christian congregation in the apostle's absence. Although we are not told why Paul should give detailed instructions to a young protégé about matters that seem obvious to others, the charge to correct certain rivals seems to make Paul's absence more threatening to a fledgling congregation. But the theological crisis that occasions this letter is not the pesky presence of rival teachers but Paul's departure from Ephesus. The difficult tasks of forming a Christian congregation in a non-Christian world are left to inexperienced Timothy. While the mention of opponents may sound an alert, the letter's real aim is to guide his successor in forming a healthy Christian congregation that continues according to the "glorious gospel of God" entrusted to the apostle Paul.

Ephesus was a cultural and religious center of the ancient world and the capital city of Roman Asia—one of the empire's most prosperous regions. Within its biblical setting, however, the letter's Ephesian address cues another portrait of Ephesus: the story of Paul's mission in Ephesus, according to Acts 19, which plots a story of a city rife with anti-Semitic conflict provoked by Paul's identity as a Jewish rabbi. Despite a mission that embraced both Jews and gentiles (cf. 19:10, 17), the congregation's dismissal from the local synagogue (cf. 19:9) and wider conflict over Paul's Jewish identity (cf. 19:34) forms an important subtext that shapes our reading of the letter's notes about the chaos caused by the opponents whom Paul dismisses as misinformed Torah teachers (cf. 1:6–11).

1. *The aim of instruction: loving relationships (1:3–5).* The hortatory *parakaleō* ("request"; 1:3) introduces a request with a note of irony since an apostolic request presumes compliance: Paul gives instructions with the air of command. Yet the apodosis of this initial and programmatic request is lacking, with the rhetorical effect—perhaps purposeful—of elevating the importance of Paul's departure. That is, his departure signals a succession of pastoral leadership in town, but it also means that Timothy is left on his own with only his mentor's written instruction to school him for the important business at hand.

The purpose clause (*hina*) states the first order of this business: "instruct certain individuals" (cf. 1:3). The meaning of *parangellō* ("instruct") in antiquity is quite elastic and its use here has been variously translated. The preference of most commentators is "command," following its meaning elsewhere in the Pauline corpus where Paul's teaching delineates a congregation's rule of faith and life (e.g., 1 Cor 11:17; 1 Thess 4:11; 2 Thess 2:4–12). The verb's repetition in 1:5 concentrates us on the principal aim of Paul's instruction, which indicates the holy end of a congregation's instruction. This includes false teachers whose curriculum and pedagogy do not produce love but chaos.

Paul says that these individuals not only promote "heretical teachings" (*heterodidaskaleō*, 1:3b) but they teach in a manner without thought or spiritual benefit. His sharp dismissal of a religious curriculum that specializes in "myths and unending family trees" (1:4a) is similar to concerns expressed by two religious contemporaries, Plutarch and Philo, both of whom described myths as "useless fabrications" (Plutarch, *Obs. Or.* 46) and "mistakes" that follow from inconclusive arguments (Philo, *Cong.* 53). The added adjective, "unending," adds that spending time on biblical genealogies (cf. Titus 1:14; 3:9) is simply unpersuasive when compared to instruction in Paul's gospel of grace (cf. 4:7; 2 Tim 4:4; Titus 1:14).

A congregation's theological instruction is a practical matter and should bring focus to its mission statement. For this reason, Paul's use of *mē . . . mēde* to connect vv. 3 and 4 ("do not teach . . . do not pay attention") sounds an alert to Timothy: do not teach unprofitable things in unproductive ways! Safeguard the core beliefs of Paul's gospel with a pedagogy that pays attention to a cultivation of the congregation's spiritual life and its ethical and political choices. It is not incidental that the summaries of Pauline teaching scattered across the letter are illustrated by personal example and punctuated by pointed exhortation: sound teaching from "the pulpit" forms a spiritually and relationally healthy congregation (see 1:11).

While obviously crucial in setting the letter's table, the precise meaning of *oikonomia theou*, "God's economy" (1:4), is notoriously difficult to pin down. The meaning of *oikonomia* doubtless follows from its root, *oikos* ("house"), and is generally thought to refer to the mundane routines of managing any household, familial or otherwise. Perhaps one hears resonances of a similar phrase, *theou oikonomos*, that Paul uses in Titus 1:7 of the congregation's *episkopos* or house administrator. The catchphrase used here, *oikonomia theou*, is probably rooted in this same soil as *oikonomos* ("steward") in Gal 4:2 to envisage the kind of relationship entered into with Jesus who "stewards" the outworking of a disciple's full salvation.

This sense squares with Paul's instructions to Timothy in this letter. They guide his theology and practices so that he is able to lead his congregation into a deeper understanding of God's stewardship of their salvation. Almost certainly this must be at the leading edge of Timothy's ministry and suggestive that Paul's exploration of the "household" metaphor for church orders is a significant political trope of a pattern of public life that is ultimately subversive of Roman rule. The images of suffering and imprisonment in 2 Timothy make clear that Rome and Christianity subscribe to opposite household visions.

The instruction of God's household trains its members at "loving relationships" (*agapē*; 1:5a); whether people love one another is a test of their theological orthodoxy (so also 1 John 4:7–8). In Pauline thought, *agapē* is not an abstracted rule of life but is the principal characteristic of a congregation's life together and is formed in the company of the indwelling Spirit (cf. Gal 5:16–26). As such, neighborly love is a marker of the congregation's life in Christ (cf. Rom 5:5; 8:35; 13:9). The triad of religious virtues—"pure heart, good conscience, earnest faith" (1:5b)—are the marks of the congregation that cultivates loving relations, not only between its members but toward outsiders as well. The integration of inward dispositions and loving practices is central to a Pauline definition of the Christian life and follows from the pattern of Jesus' moral instruction exemplified by Matthew's Sermon on the Mount (Matt 5:17–48; 6:1–21).

The first quality is a "pure heart" (cf. 2 Tim 2:22), which according to Jewish psychology is the epicenter of human existence: one's "heartfelt" emotions, affections, motives determine what one sees and how one acts.

Added to this are the Jewish purity laws that publicly expressed a community's covenant fellowship with God. Of course, the question of purity is central to the discussion and decision of the Jerusalem Council in Acts 15, which was prompted by the Christ-following Pharisees' question about purity and table fellowship (Acts 15:5)—a question that Peter answered by defining purity as a matter of the heart (Acts 15:6–10).

The pivotal element of this triad is the "good conscience," which is central to a Hellenistic conception of the moral life. This belief that the Creator builds into every person an internal moral apparatus shaped a Jewish (and so Paul's) moral understanding. Even though unmentioned in the synagogue's Bible, rabbi Philo listed the "good conscience" among his *Special Laws* (1:203) as the internal spiritual capacity to discern God's will with the intention of obeying it.

The final element of the triad is a "sincere faith," which adds a distinctively Christian dimension to the sort of person who has the capacity for loving relationships. Different connotations have been made of Paul's use of "faith" in the PE; however, its repetition in this passage (1:2, 4, 5) seems to imply the community's firm affirmation of God's way of stewarding the world (so 1:4b). Whether personified by the faithful actions it takes in life or in the profession of its core beliefs, the force of this virtue is the community's vigorous and rigorous embrace of the gospel truth disclosed in Christ Jesus. Augustine writes that "if our faith involves no lie, then we do not love that which is not to be loved, and living justly, we hope for that which will in no way deceive our hope" (*On Christian Doctrine* 1:40–44).

2. *Building a healthy congregation (1:10–11).* According to the PE, what conforms to "the glorious gospel of the blessed God" (1:11) in life and doctrine is considered theologically "healthy" (1:10; *hygiaineō*)—a Greek medical term that provides an apt metaphor of the good effect of Christian instruction (cf. 1 Tim 6:3; 2 Tim 1:13; 4:3; Titus 1:9, 13; 2:1–2). This adjective evokes the image of a vital congregation shaped by Pauline instruction and would have struck a responsive chord among its ancient readers who were familiar with its use in moral discourse: good instruction is the moral foundation of all healthy relationships. Maximus of Tyre wrote a century after Paul that "truth and healthy understanding and morality and knowledge of the law and right cannot be acquired in any other way than by actually doing them, just as one can never learn the craft of shoemaking unless one actually works at it" (*Discourses* 16.3).

The spiritual health of a Christian congregation and its leadership is the salutary effect of the orthodoxy of its instruction. Paul's is a practical divinity, always expressed in terms that connect the proclamation of truth with how truth performs in real life. For this reason, loving relations between people spring forth from those inward dispositions forged by a healthy doctrine; and an "unlawful" use of the law (cf. 1:8) is that brittle kind of legalism that substitutes a rigorous doing the law's letter for a robust dependence upon divine grace.

Expression of thanksgiving for another is a standard, although not uniform, ingredient of Pauline letters. In most cases, epistolary thanksgivings function much like a pastoral prayer, when thanksgiving is given and petitions offered to God for the wellbeing of the audience. In this case, however, Paul thanks Jesus for saving him from ignorance and unbelief (1:13) and for a ministry of the gospel entrusted to him (1:11–12). This combination of conversion and commission is imagined as a pouring out of divine grace (1:14) to demonstrate to others not only that "Christ Jesus came into the world to save sinners" (1:15–16) but also that such a salvation does not follow a conventional pattern of human existence but is the merciful effect of the one and only God (1:17).

Unlike his other letters, however, Paul's thanksgiving is biographical (*charin echō . . . me*, lit. "I thank . . . me"). Its purpose is to explain the theological centerpiece of the gospel entrusted to Paul (1:10–11), which is the religious experience of a sinner's conversion from ignorance and unbelief. If this biography of conversion is contextualized by a prior reading of its narration in Acts, the reader more easily notes that the drama of Paul's conversion (cf. Acts 9:1–9) is decisively linked to his missionary calling (cf. Acts 9:15–16; 26:15–18). Paul's conversion is a teachable moment that not only shapes his gospel message about the salvation-creating power of God's grace but underwrites Christ's appointment to his apostleship as well (cf. Gal 1:11–17). Here, as in Acts, Paul's conversion stages his commission and is, then, the most decisive moment of his ministry of the gospel.

3. *Paul as exemplary of the "glorious gospel" of God's grace (1:12–17)*. The irony presented by Pauline biography is that these snapshots of an apostle's life are not really about Paul but about all those others whose similar experiences of a responsible grace frame their reading of Paul's testimony. His biography, especially when contextualized by the conversion narratives of Acts (chs. 9, 22, 26), stipulates a core belief that regulates any theological reading of Pauline letters and also personifies a normative pattern of

the transforming effect of grace in all matters of life (cf. 1:17). The phrase translated "this teaching is a core belief" (*pistos ho logos*; 1:15) appears five times in the PE (1 Tim 1:15; 3:1; 4:9; 2 Tim 2:11; Titus 3:8; cf. Titus 1:9) and nowhere else in the NT. In each case, the phrase either introduces or concludes a Pauline formulation of God's way of salvation. Regarding this saying, "Christ Jesus came into the world to save sinners" summarizes what is found in the "glorious gospel" entrusted to him (1:10–11) and is what one scholar has called a Pauline "creedal cameo."[1] How these catchphrases originated is difficult to determine; they were likely created, however, as missionary "soundbites"—memorable yet dense phrases that helped converts conceptualize their experience of being initiated into Christian faith.

The spiritual crisis that requires such a conversion is the sinner's ignorance of God's redemptive purpose, and so agrees with how sin is routinely understood in Hellenistic Judaism (cf. Josephus, *Ant.* 3.231–32). The theme of human active ignorance of divine providence is also a narrative theme of Acts (Acts 3:17; 17:3). Reading Acts prior to this letter secures more firmly this theological point: God gives second chances to those whose prior rejection of God's Messiah is a matter of their ignorance of scripture's messianic way of salvation rather than a matter of bad character. In this case, the attentive hearing of God's glorious gospel may dispel one's ignorance and open up one's heart to knowledge of God's truth (cf. 1 Tim 2:4).

Even though "Christ Jesus" is the name used for Jesus in PE, here Paul adds "our Lord." The public profession that the risen Jesus is the church's Lord is a principal identity marker of Pauline congregations in the public square (cf. Rom 10:9). By this public profession of faith, sinners admit their agreement with the central claims of Paul's gospel about Christ's atoning death, bodily resurrection, heavenly exaltation, and triumphant return (see 3:16). That is, all believers share with the apostle the same core beliefs about Christ and experience the same realization that Jesus "came into the world to save sinners . . . for eternal life."

The concluding doxology (1:17) is characteristically Pauline, especially since it reflects upon the apostle's own strategic role within the global economy of God's salvation (Rom 11:36; Gal 1:5; Eph 3:20–21). The terms of his praise size up the character of the One who has the capacity to make good on the stunning promise to save sinners for eternal life through Christ Jesus. This general depiction of deity to underwrite his more particularly Christian claim about Jesus has a familiar ring in both Hellenistic and Jewish worlds

---

1. Collins, *1 & 2 Timothy and Titus*, 43.

and this is precisely its purpose here, which envisages the formation of a Christian congregation, microscopic of the *oikonomia theou*, in a pagan world: to invite a conversation between these two worlds about God's manner of saving people from self-destructive sins through Christ.

Preaching 1 Timothy 1

Let me introduce the prospect of preaching or teaching Paul's PE by stating again the primary problem of how to translate our exegesis for a congregation or classroom setting. How do Paul's exhortations or instructions to Timothy apply to us all? Our work with the PE requires two, not simply one level of imagination. First, we must think analogically and imagine what relevance Paul's communication to Timothy about his ministry in the "strange world" of ancient Ephesus has for today's readers and their social worlds? This is what scripture's interpretation always requires of its readers, even those who were next in line after Timothy to reread Paul's correspondence in another congregation down the Roman highway from Ephesus. But, second, we must also imagine what relevance Paul's communication to an individual, Timothy or Titus, has for an entire congregation or classroom of students. Based upon a close reading of what Paul writes in these letters, then, we must do our best to imagine and then translate how Timothy or Titus would relate Paul's teaching to their own parishes for our own day, for the people under our care.

One of the benefits of preaching the Pastorals is that it has an abundance of soundbites that make great sermon points. In fact, throughout this commentary, I will use these pithy sayings—perhaps preformed and recycled by Paul in these letters because they were familiar and understood—to cue and even organize sketches of my sermon ideas.

Sermon big idea

Paul begins this letter as he often does by stating a problem: there are teachers of false ideas and conspiracy theories who may have influenced the congregation Timothy is delegated to pastor under Paul's apostolic umbrella. This conflict is only rarely absent from any congregation. There will always be alternatives to the gospel's truth that influence how believers think about and embody their witness as disciples of the risen Jesus. Whether we are always aware of the influence of these opponents, especially now that social media often carry their "heretical" freight near and far, the public identity of a congregation and the mission that states who they are and what they do is hammered out in part fully wakeful that our congregations live in a world populated with alternatives to the gospel and God's way of salvation.

In response, the opening charge for Timothy to "fight the good fight" (1:18) provides Timothy with a mission statement. Perhaps it has to do with the present cultural moment in which we live, but increasing attention is being paid to mission statements of organizations and sharply worded descriptions of their public identity or "brand." This seems especially true of nonprofit, voluntary organizations such as Christian congregations and church-related universities and their seminaries. To some extent, this effort is public relations: how does the church meet the culture and what is the benefit of its ministry within and for the good of the whole neighborhood? But the most important reason for spending time crafting a mission statement or the "who are we and what do we do?" profile we post on our church's webpage is self-understanding. The ministries of our congregation or the so-called "learning outcomes" of the courses we teach in seminary are to a very large extent shaped by the aims and purposes of our existence as a people belonging to God.

Sermon sketch

Three soundbites retrieved from this passage may provide the talking points in crafting a sermon or lesson that offers a congregation of parishioners or students a compelling mission statement that engages the world with the gospel's truth.

1. *"The aim of our instruction is loving relationships"* (1:4). Begin by setting out the aim of a congregation whose mission is right on target. Paul tells Timothy that the "aim" or *telos* of his gospel is love (1:5). Notice how I define Paul's use of this idea in his letters: *agapē* ("love") is not an abstracted rule of life but is the principal characteristic of a congregation's life together and is formed in the company of the indwelling Spirit. While a congregation's mission is to form a community that enjoys each other's company—a "life together" in which members take responsibility for the care and wellbeing of other members—it always does so in the company of the Spirit who forms those inward dispositions of the heart and mind that order this life together by loving relationships.

Paul's response to the fuss provoked by the teaching of fake news is not to counter with instruction of good news. Yes, he tells Timothy to correct the falsehoods being taught; his primary move, however, is to list the inward marks of the Spirit's indwelling presence by a triad of dispositions: "pure heart," "good conscience," and "sincere faith." The formulation of a congregation's mission statement that follows this passage should center on the importance of a shared life of loving relationships but make clear in doing so that such a social life is the result of a commitment to congregational practices of the spiritual disciplines—prayer for one another, worship with one another, targeted Bible study—that animate the Spirit's cultivation of those habits of a pure heart, good conscience, and sincere faith that form the capacity to love one another.

2. *Live a healthy teaching that accords with "the glorious gospel of God" (1:10b–11).* What makes for a "healthy" congregation? The church multiplies divisions. There is hardly a season that passes without some news report of a congregation or denomination divided over a belief or practice. This sad reality is the opposite of the church of Acts, whose narrative of mission and congregational formation establishes the norm for today's church. Today's church bears little similarity to Jerusalem's congregation of those first believers, who were "of one heart and soul" (Acts 4:32). We are a body of Christ in poor health with a lot of broken bones. A mission statement should provide a vision of healing what is broken and a prognosis of health for its future.

While Paul's initial exhortation to Timothy targeted loving relationships ordered by Spirit-animated practices of the heart and soul, he turns quickly to the teaching of the "glorious gospel" that promote the health of a congregation (1:10b–11). Every mission statement should include a grammar of faith—the primary nouns and verbs that we consider indispensable in our life with God and comprise the way we testify our experiences of God's way of salvation that have liberated us from the evils that hobble human existence.

3. *Paul was treated with mercy, making him an example of those who believe in Jesus Christ (1:12–17). Conversion of the Imagination* is the title of a collection of important essays on biblical interpretation written by Richard B. Hays, among America's finest interpreters of Paul. This title signals an attractive way of thinking about a holy end of how followers of Jesus come to read their world by the light of scripture. The Greek word for "repentance" (*metanoeō*) literally means a "transformation (*meta-*) of

understanding (*noeō*)." The mark of those who repent and turn to Jesus is a transformed understanding of their lives and the worlds in which they live. Paul speaks negatively of the "teachers of the Torah" (1:7) who "do not understand (*noeō*) what they are saying." Central to Paul's self-understanding of his conversion is his own transformation from "the worst of sinners" (1:15), who acted "arrogantly and ignorantly in unbelief" as a "blasphemer and persecutor" (1:13), to someone who proclaimed and lived according to the "glorious gospel of God" (1:11). Conversion provided him with a new rationalism, a different theo-logic that enables him to see Christ, people, the world through the lens of grace.

There are many reasons why this passage is lifted up as among the most important descriptions of Paul's spiritual life in his letters and Acts. Students and parishioners should be made aware of the history of its interpretation in both the church and academy. I understand the power of personal testimony; it has always been among the most important practices of Methodist worship. John Wesley founded Methodism during the beginnings of England's reception of the Enlightenment and its turn toward hard evidence to secure our claims about truth. Public testimony in which converts gave details, often sordid and sometimes salacious, of their turn from sin to holiness provided people with a good reason to consider Christianity. When this passage is read by the stories of Paul's conversion to the risen Jesus in Acts, we understand its apologetical value. Here is a personal testimony to the healing effect of accepting the truth that "Christ Jesus came into the world to save sinners" that demonstrates it for all to see.

More importantly, it provides the organizing center of the "glorious gospel" that was entrusted to Paul (1:11): the abundance of the Lord's grace (1:14) that treats the sinner with mercy, patience, and kindness. A congregation must be a people who make this point crystal clear in the grammar that communicates their faith to others. But the congregation must also be a people who can provide examples or testimonies of their ministry of grace at work in meeting the challenges that face all of us the public square but also in the lives and relationships of those members who make up the congregation.

Chapter 2

A CONGREGATION'S WORSHIP PRACTICES

Exegetical Notes on 1 Timothy 2

PAUL'S INSTRUCTION TO TIMOTHY in this chapter seeks to bring clarity to the theological motive and social manners of Christian worship. He covers the three core practices of Christian worship: prayers for everyone (2:1–4), confession of faith (2:5–7), and the social manners and public gestures of orderly worship (2:8—3:1a).

1. *The practice of prayer (2:1–4).* Paul frames his instructions about prayers—among the longest and most detailed descriptions in the NT—by implicating two different and often competing households: the political household led by "kings and those in positions of authority" (2:2; cf. Titus 3:1–2) and the religious household led by God. Paul recognizes the tension often provoked among and within believers between these rival households. This tension seems especially clear today in American life. The relationship between the holy ends of the congregation's prayers (2:3–4) and their confession of faith (2:5–7) settle this tension theologically: a congregation's politics serve the *missio Dei* not only by leading a "peaceable and calm life" (2:2) but also by petitioning God to save everyone, "even the kings," from death (2:4) for a shared life with God, the one and only "eternal King" (so 1:16–17).

Paul's instruction on prayer is placed "first of all" in importance (2:1). The opening "therefore" probably assumes a contrast between false teachers (1:3–11, 19–20) and the apostle whose own conversion from falsehood imitates prophetic ministry (1:12–17; cf. 2:7). But Paul's emphasis on congregational prayer is a means of peacekeeping with everyone (2:2), including his opponents.

Two brief observations about the importance of congregational prayers guide the interpretation of this passage. First, God's household must be ordered to serve God's redemptive purposes. The universal scope of the congregation's prayers is in line with the universal scope of God's desire to save everyone and effect of Christ's atoning sacrifice. The content and motive of prayers to God should seek what God seeks.

The phrase "rulers and all those in positions of authority" is added as an irony since most scholars agree these instructions were given at a historical moment when Rome allowed the persecution of believers in certain regions of the empire. Christians who confess belief in the sovereignty of one God and the lordship of one Lord, Christ Jesus, challenged the central ideological tenet of the empire: the sovereign rule of its emperor. The sociopolitical friction that resulted between a powerless church and a powerful state is found everywhere in the NT (e.g., Acts 22–28; 1 Pet 3:13–17; Rev 13). Even though counterintuitive, the instruction to pray for and support those leading the secular household was widely shared in antiquity. Paul's Judaism practiced praying for one's pagan rulers, following the example of Daniel, who used prayer to ensure peaceful relationships with hostile pagan powers. Early Christians followed their Jewish ancestors in contending for a deep solidarity with their sociopolitical world as a faithful response to the Creator's provident care for all things.[1]

Second, if the ultimate outcome of a congregation's worship is to testify to its membership in God's household, then the subject matter of its prayers and petitions must support the redemptive activities of God in the world. Worship is a verbal noun precisely because its practices demonstrate a community's loyalty to God. With a social setting where the two households, secular and sacred, are sometimes in conflict, public prayers may be seen as a radical, countercultural, and demonstrative activity. A people's worship practices are a principal means by which that group embodies its allegiance to God and its vocation to reorder the empire after God's will.

1. Johnson, *Delegates*, 129–31.

The use of the word *basileus* ("king") repeats the doxological refrain just heard in the letter's thanksgiving, where God is honored as immortal *basileus* (1:17), a trope that is repeated at the end of the letter, where God is declared "the King of the kings" (6:15). This doxological envelope not only underwrites the church's confession of a sovereign God but sets the congregation's prayers within the political boundaries of the economy of divine love. The ambivalence of praying to Creation's King of kings for the empire's kings is quite arresting, if only because petitions about kings and lords are received by a God who knows what it takes to be a righteous king.

Paul's principal motive that prompts and concentrates the congregation's prayers is clearly theological: to pray for everybody is to pray for what God desires most: salvation from sin made possible by coming to a knowledge of the truth (2:4). Prayers for the emperor, which routinely offered petitions for his personal safety and political wisdom, finally were offered to God in prospect of the emperor's conversion to the truth and the empire's salvation from its evils.

Much has been made of the purpose (*hina*) clause that follows the instruction to pray for kings, which some take as indication that such prayers serve a political end—keeping the peace and avoiding protest—as an accommodation to the social order of the empire. But if the congregation's prayers are interpreted by the following Pauline formula of *missio Dei*, then the purpose of prayer is to produce a material result in the public square. That is, Christians pray for the salvation of our leaders so that their decisions and actions have a salutary effect on the public order. The combination of the adjectives *ēremos* ("peaceable") with *ēsychios* ("quiet") is not a redundancy, as is often suggested, but mutually glossing expressions that combine internal and personal with external and social experiences of God's shalom to indicate the full salvation of everyone and everything. Civil religion, no; missional church, yes.

2. *The practice of confessions of faith (2:5–7).* The compressed theological formula in verses 5–6, perhaps preformed and known to Timothy, elaborates the final phrase of verse 4: this confession of faith defines the "truth" that once known and owned is the means of receiving God's saving grace. This is the narrative of salvation that measures all other narratives of salvation and exposes them as fake rather than good news. Given the variety of conspiracies and false narratives that abound in today's culture wars, this same question should be asked today. The passages in Titus 2–3 considered in this commentary make it clear that the task of Christian

education and the missional church is truth-telling and the church's bold articulation of truth is set out in the essential elements of the creed Paul inserts in his instructions of worship.

(1) "There is one God." Any theism must begin with an affirmation that one and only one God truly exists. Such a belief is not seditious nor is it the practice of a domesticated church. It more simply stipulates that one Creator God's plan to save everyone and everything, seen and unseen, is singular and definitive.

(2) "There is one mediator between God and humankind." Paul's insistence on a single way of salvation continues with his affirmation that there is but one who mediates God's salvation, Christ Jesus. One God, one Messiah, one salvation forms a grammar of God's economy of grace: God's offer of universal salvation is tendered by a single ambassador; to receive it from any other source on any other grounds is bogus.

(3) "A man, Christ Jesus." The reference to Jesus' humanity seems awkward at first. Some suggest that it goes best with the next phrase, which speaks of Jesus' death. Paul's exhortation for Timothy to "remember Jesus Christ, raised from the dead, a descendant of David" (2 Tim 2:8) sums up his gospel and probably is in play here as well: the human Jesus was executed by Rome and the crucified Jesus was raised from the dead by God. Moreover, if God desires every human to come to a knowledge of the gospel's truth, then the incarnation of God's Son as Messiah Jesus makes crystal clear God's desire to save every one of us.

(4) "[Christ Jesus] who gave himself a ransom for everybody." In Paul's social world, payment of a "ransom" freed slaves from indenture; and perhaps the most important biblical typology of God's way of salvation is God's liberation of an enslaved Israel from its captivity to a pagan power to live in its land and freely worship its God. The politics of worship, which supplies an important subtext to the present instructions, is shaped not by Rome but by this exodus story. Yet Timothy may well have expected a more traditional Pauline dogmatics: "who gave himself a ransom for sin" (cf. Titus 2:14). Instead, Paul repeats "for all" (2:1) because under the present circumstances he is pressing for an inclusive scope of God's way of salvation to motivate the congregation to pray for the salvation of even its pagan, oppressive rulers. Sharply put, Christians pray for everybody because Christ died for everybody in agreement with God's chief desire to save everybody.

Paul's mention of payment of a "ransom" to liberate those captivated by sin would have special currency in Roman Ephesus with its huge slave population and so could have evoked images of the price paid to set a slave free. Furthermore, the prefix Paul adds to the common word for "ransom" (*lytron*), *anti-* ("instead"), produces a more nuanced idea of the payment made that Jesus exchanged his human life to save everyone else (*antilytron*). The very idea of a person substituting his life for a community or nation is the noblest definition of covenant loyalty in the holy texts of Paul's Judaism (see 4 Macc 6:29; 17:21–22; 2 Macc 7:37–38; cf. Deut 32:36; Mark 10:45).

(5) Paul "was appointed a herald, an apostle . . . , and a teacher of the nations in matters of faith and truth" (1 Tim 2:7). The apostle's reference to himself as appointed by God to herald the good news to the nations (cf. 1:1) suggests his sense of an ambassadorial role: he serves as Christ's "under-secretary" who is given the task of communicating God's gospel in Christ's personal absence. There may well be an even deeper implication that now in Paul's absence Timothy is given this crucial task to perform in Ephesus.

The idealized character of Paul's apostleship is a central concern of the PE, not in his defense, as in other Pauline letters (e.g., Galatians, 2 Corinthians, Romans), but rather to underwrite a canonical Paul whose memory and message passed on by scripture's canonical collection of his letters are considered exemplary for future generations of believers. Nowhere else in scripture is found this stunning claim that Paul's apostolic mission is to herald and teach God's singular truth to the nations. A prior reading of Paul's story in Acts—following the natural flow of the NT—would prime the reader to understand Paul's use of "nations" in this missional formula in its most inclusive sense: to the Jew first (so Acts 1–9) and then to the non-Jew (so Acts 10–28). The canonical Paul targets the same population group that concentrates the worshiping community's prayers: *everybody* (cf. Acts 9:15). Any collision, not collusion, between the apostolic herald and the nations results from Paul's demand of a singular faith and the unsettling truth about God's economy of salvation, which are at the messy epicenter of every culture war of every generation.

3. *The practice of orderly worship (2:8–14).* While Paul's understanding of his mission to the nations follows the commission of Matthew's Jesus to make disciples of all nations (Matt 28:19), the instructions aimed at worshiping men and women that follow are "therefore" (2:8) embodiments of Paul's mission statement (2:7). In particular, the profiles of Christian men who pray with uplifted hands "in every place" as a public gesture of their intention to lead peaceable and godly lives (cf. 2:2b) along with virtuous

Christian women supply examples to copy of the transforming power of God's grace with a positive effect wherever they live.

Most modern interpreters understand that these instructions recalibrate well-known caricatures of competitive men and modest women found in Greco-Roman literature, transforming them into idealized exemplars of the faith. Paul nowhere refers to specific individuals by name nor to problems that they provoke within the Ephesian culture or their Christian congregations. The purpose of his instruction is to provide general patterns of daily practice that serve God's redemptive purpose. Such practices are as much acts of worship as their prayers. Moreover, the connecting *hōsautōs* ("likewise," 2:9) indicates that women (or wives) share equally with men (or husbands) in the congregation's public worship and share equally the demands of orderly public conduct (cf. 1 Cor 11:4–5).

Of course, the book of Acts already alerts readers that Paul's mission in urban centers of the Roman world attracted accomplished women who sometimes came from upper-class Roman households. Paul's expansive instructions in this passage recognize that their turn to Jesus was embodied by manners apropos of their elevated social status and finances, whether by their appearance (2:9), their philanthropic works (2:10), or their schooling (2:11–12). It is a mistake to read his instructions out of cultural context or attentiveness to a mission that aligns with "God our Savior who desires to save all people" (2:3–4). Moreover, the story of Priscilla's important ministry in Timothy's Ephesus, according to Acts 18:18–28, especially when combined with Paul's "Magna Carta" in Gal 3:28 and biblical portraits of women prophets (e.g., Huldah) and witnesses (e.g., Samaritan woman of John 4), resist any attempt to absolutize this single text as normative for all time zones and zip codes.

In any case, the various marks of the ideal Christian woman unfold within a rhetorical unit bracketed by the repetition of "prudence" (*sōphrosynē*) (2:9, 15), the most admired female virtue of the age. Paul also uses *sōphrosynē* as characteristic of any Christian leader, male or female (see 3:2; cf. Titus 1:8; 2:2, 5; cf. Acts 26:25). In this sense, the prudence of Christian women is not gendered but embodies the character of any mature Jesus follower who "abstains from whatever tends to sin" (Tertullian, *On the Apparel of Women*, 2:2). What is clearly more important than gender is social class. Paul's instructions target a certain class of women with time and money to dress well, to engage in philanthropic works, and to be schooled by private tutors. These are the most prominent women of Ephesian society and attention is paid to them and their social manners.

The implied contrast between secular and women of "religious piety" (*theosebeia*, 2:10) is well known from antiquity. Stoic philosophers wrote of the trivial pursuits of secular women who lacked moral scruples in their pursue of material things and personal appearance. On the other hand, religious women were observably concerned with the well-being of others and were thought to exemplify "a life of productive virtue."[2] In modern parlance, prudence may seem like such a pale platitude. But in classical culture, prudence embodied a thoughtful wisdom and street savvy. If prudent practices exhibit self-possession and a competent dignity of women known for their know-how, then "prudence" may lose some of its current Victorian distastefulness. Put differently, Paul may be drawing, as he did often in crafting the paraenetic sections of his letters, on Second Temple Judaism's (STJ) wisdom tradition and its conception of *hokmah*—a skill for living well—in describing the competent woman who followed Christ rather than the norms of pagan culture, considered by Stoics as banal.

More recently, a religious woman's public identity is sometimes linked to her stylish dress (2:9). Pentecostal scholar Leah Payne has made a persuasive case for the importance of the sometimes extravagant dress of women preachers in symbolizing their powerful and public role performed during the early formative period of American Pentecostalism.[3] Conversely women of my own Methodist church of the same period refused to wear jewelry or expensive clothing to "dress down" in order to form an otherwise unnatural solidarity with the poor and powerless.

Moreover, the importance of practicing "good works" (2:10) is repeatedly mentioned in the PE; these are works that God wills and become, then, the hallmark of mature believers (cf. 2 Tim 3:17). Because the practice of

---

2. Johnson, *The First and Second Letters to Timothy*, 204–8.

3. Payne, *Gender and Pentecostal Revivalism*. The relevance of Payne's historical work for preaching this text is its offering of a possible contemporary (and entertaining!) analogy to the Ephesian setting of 1 Timothy where women connected to the city's popular Artemis shrine engaged in various kinds of religious practices; see Hoag, *Wealth in Ancient Ephesus and the First Letter to Timothy*. If Artemis was worshiped as a goddess of fertility, these religious practices may have included childbirth, which provides a reason for Paul's mention of "childbearing" in 1 Tim 2:15a, although I doubt it (see below). See, however, the recent book by Sandra Glahn, *Nobody's Mother: Artemis of the Ephesians in Antiquity and the New Testament*, which adds helpful background against which the intended meaning of Paul's puzzling (and contested) phrase that "the woman is saved through childbearing" (2:15a) may be made clearer.

good works is evident to all (so 1 Tim 5:25), they are a good describer of the social manners of Christian women because their doing of God's work proves useful in persuading outsiders in God's direction. While doing "good works" (2:10) is "evident" to all (1 Tim 5:25) they are a social marker (cf. 5:10, 25; 6:18–20) that provides evidence of Christianity's positive effect on society—a persuasive societal standard for a newly introduced religion (cf. Acts 17:18–31) and reconceived in 1 Timothy as another concrete witness to the transforming power of divine mercy (cf. 1:12–16).

The most expansive demonstration of female prudence, however, applies to a theme of primary importance in this letter: from whom and in what manner should a Christian congregation learn the truth of God's way of salvation. Paul applies this general concern in a personal admonition that Christian women learn in "full submission" and actively "attentive" (*ēsychios*, cf. 2:2) to their tutors. This instruction is not exceptional; it is true of all believers, as is made clear in almost every section of the PE. This is essential to the orderly worship of God's people. The pronounced shift from third-person to first-person voice in verse 12 and from a general exhortation to personal injunction that begins (*ouk epitrepō*: "I do not allow," 2:12) underscores the apostle's sense of its practical importance in guiding the social manners of exemplary women in the economy of the *missio Dei*.[4]

Preachers today must handle this text with considerable care; indeed, they may never care to preach it! Almost certainly, however, they will need to respond to its present use by some as a "text of terror" whose misuse has been deeply troubling for an increasing number of women who are called, gifted, and trained for Christian ministry but are then silenced by their church's application of this single passage. The purpose of this exegetical note is to offer another way of reading this text that agrees with the non-gendered tenor of Paul's entire apostolic witness received with his canonical letters and story in Acts.

Further, the preachers should resist any "mirror reading" of this text that imagines Paul's instructions seek to correct a "female problem" in Timothy's Ephesian congregation; there is no evidence anywhere in 1 Timothy that such a problem existed. Most scholars think the mention of "immature women" in 2 Tim 3:6–7 is an element among many of the apocalypticized polemics that envision the "last days" (3:1) populated

---

4. For a more detailed exposition of this passage, so central in the contemporary debate over women in ministry, see my commentary on *1 & 2 Timothy and Titus*, 85–98, 174–77, 188–90.

with "people" (2 Tim 3:2) who have the public "form" of Christian piety without its transforming "power" (3:5) and who, like Jannes and Jambres, "oppose the truth" (3:8). In this setting, Paul intends the picture he draws to function as a counterexample for the sort of spiritual leader Timothy must become, according to the following triad of exhortations that begin with "But you . . ." (3:10, 14; 4:5).

Among those mentioned in this population to avoid are people who prey on women "overwhelmed with sins" who "seek instruction but never come to a knowledge of the truth" (3:7). While Paul's evident purpose here is rhetorical and hortatory and does not seek to correct an actual incident occurring in Timothy's congregation, it has relevance for an interpretation of Paul's motive for his use of Eve's story in 1 Timothy: Paul's concern is for attentive learning of truth and resistance to those "various passions" (3:6) that deflect it. This is not a gendered concern of his, even though he uses culturally shaped examples of virtuous women (1 Tim 2:11–12) and "immature women" (2 Tim 3:6–7) to express it, but the exhortation for attentive learning of the gospel's truth is found in every one of his canonical letters.[5] In this setting in 1 Timothy, however, his instructions for the attentive learning of upper-class women of the Ephesian congregation reflects a missional concern to provide all people with the truth of God's way of salvation so that in coming to a knowledge of its claims all people might turn to a God who is the Savior of all people.

The history of interpreting Eve's story in 1 Tim 2:13–15a tends to focus on Paul's initial observation from Genesis 2 that "Adam was formed first then Eve" (2:13). The plausible deduction is typically made that this element of his rereading of Torah features a claim of male priority in both the classroom and the pulpit (cf. 1 Cor 11:8–9). More difficult in my view is understanding Paul's next observation that while Adam was not deceived, Eve was and she "fell into sin" as a result (2:14). Especially when read in canonical context, it would seem impossible logic to then argue that an undeceived Adam did not follow a deceived Eve into sin (cf. Rom 5:12). Nowhere does Paul elevate Adam as a sinless exemplar of truthtelling! Both Adam and Eve are Pauline types of human sinners in need of God's saving grace.

What is notably distinctive about a fallen Eve when compared with a fallen Adam is that her sin follows from her deception. Nowhere does Paul mention "deception" in his use of an Adam typology in Romans 5

5. Campbell, *Pauline Dogmatics*, 198–205.

or 1 Corinthians 15, and he plainly eliminates it in his retelling of Eve's story in 1 Timothy 2: "Adam was not deceived" (*apataō*, 2:14a). This too follows closely the biblical narrative since it was Eve but not Adam who confesses her "deception" by the tricky serpent to God (Gen 3:13). In light of this comparison, I propose a reading of Paul's retelling of Eve's story in 1 Timothy that does not focus on the priority of Adam's creation but rather on making better sense of the nature of Eve's "deception." This would seem to hold the more critical clue for understanding Paul's unwritten motive for including her story, namely, to secure his admonition that the ideal Christian woman "must remain attentive" to her teachers so that God's desire that all people come to a knowledge of the truth may be realized.

According to Eve's biblical story in Genesis 2, it is true that her creation follows Adam's. The close reader will note in canonical context, however, that according to the initial story of human creation in Genesis 1:27–28, male and female are created at the same time and together receive the same command from the Creator to "increase, multiply, and fill the earth." Nonetheless, even Adam's priority in the sequence of scripture's second creation story raises numerous problems, all of which are settled in the storyteller's verdict that "It is not good that Adam is alone" (Gen 2:18). God's response to Adam's aloneness is to then form Eve.

One of the implied obligations facing the once single Adam is to instruct Eve what God had commanded him, prior to Eve's creation, about the fruit of Eden's trees (Gen 2:16–17). Evidently, he had done so because Eve was able to respond to the serpent's opening question about God's earlier instruction to Adam (Gen 3:1b); she would not have been able to do so without Adam's instruction. But it is her response to the trickster's question of this instruction that gave it the opening that pressured his deception of Eve. According to some rabbis, perhaps a midrash known to Paul, the serpent recognized Eve's culpability for deception when she misquoted God's instruction to Adam, replying that God commanded them not even to touch the fruit of the tree for knowing good and evil (Gen 3:3; cf. 2:17).[6]

Sharply put, this emphasis on Eve's deception by Eden's serpent may be understood as the result of her inattentiveness to Adam's instruction of God's commandment about the fruit tree in the middle of the garden. Paul's phrase that "Adam was formed first, then Eve," then, might rather be read *not* as a trope of male priority in the church's teaching office but rather as relating to the circumstance of his reception of God's commandment that

---

6. See, e.g., Jon Levenson's notes on Gen 2:15–4:2 in *The Jewish Study Bible*, 16–18.

only he received and of his subsequent instruction of the woman formed after him. This reading of Eve's creation story makes better sense as an elaboration of Paul's admonition in 2:12 since it coheres more closely to the general interest of the PE in a healthy theological formation that must resist the teaching of "deceiving spirits" (1 Tim 4:1) in a congregation's coming to "believe and know the truth" (4:3).

This idea is not isolated to the PE but receives support from Jas 1:25–27, where this same verb for being "deceived" (*apataō*, 1:26) is used to characterize the inattentive or "forgetful" listener of God's "perfect law of liberty" (1:25)—a lack of learning that results in "deception" and then in an ineffective, impure religion (1:26). In this same way, Eve's inattention to Adam's instruction of God's law led to her deception by the serpent and finally to her transgression. Further, this sort of religion is unable to care for widows (cf. 1 Tim 5:3–16) or keep from being contaminated by the surrounding culture (1:26–27; cf. 2 Tim 3:1–9).

4. *She will be saved through childbearing (2:15—3:1a).* This brings us to 1 Tim 2:15, which remains "one of the strangest verses in the New Testament."[7] This "strangeness" is doubtless due in part to the editorial work of later scribes who divided Paul's letters into chapters and verses, separating his retelling of Eve's fall into sin (2:13–14) from the phrase that quite likely notes her eschatological salvation: "she will be saved, however, through childbearing" (2:15a). The result of doing so effectively disrupts the theo-logic of Eve's story: she is left in verse 14 as a type of sinner whose deception exposes a propensity to sin if left without the covering of strong male leader-ship—even though the biblical Adam hardly provides a role model for this sort of leader! In any case, readers are left to linger with the Eve of 2:13–14, typological of a deceived woman in need of male headship, whether in the church or at home, to whom she must be "completely submissive" and to whose instruction she must quietly receive. If readers, however, approach Paul's story of Eve in context, not only of his profile of the virtuous Christian woman whose dress, deeds, and decorum are motivated by the *missio Dei* (2:3–6), then they are more likely to end her story where Paul does, not with sin and death but rather with salvation and life.

There are (at least) three exegetical issues to settle in interpreting this strange phrase, "but she will be saved through childbearing" (2:15a). (1) The first is to determine the subject of the third person singular verb of *sōzō* (*she* will be saved). It seems difficult to think it is linked to the

---

7. Mounce, *Pastoral Epistles*, 143.

conditional that follows because of the latter's pluriformed verbal idea, "if *they* remain in faith, love, and holiness" (2:15b). The most natural way grammatically to identify the woman who will be saved is that she is the one just mentioned: Eve. This also is the most natural way for Paul to conclude any individual's story of salvation since his confession and motivation for mission is that "God our Savior desires all people to be saved" (2:4). (2) The second task, then, is to understand the future tense of *sōzō* (she *will be* saved): in what sense does Eve's story conclude in the future? The future passive of *sōzō* expresses the consummation of God's salvation that Eve's story prefigures. Salvation does, of course, have a present tense too: we experience God's saving grace that relieves us of sin's guilt and transforms our minds and hearts in solidarity with the living Christ. But salvation also has a future tense when God's promise of eternal life will have its full and final realization. This is what the forgiven Eve awaits, along with all those who trust in God our Savior. (3) Perhaps the most demanding exegetical problem—and certainly the one that has attracted the most attention during the long history of its reception—is the agency of Eve's salvation: "childbearing" (*teknogonia*), a word used only here in scripture. Given my argument that this phrase concludes Eve's story of salvation, the question is in what sense does Eve's "childbearing" save her?

The answer may be found in the opening of humanity's post-Eden story in Genesis 4. Following God's judgment of Eve's sin and her prescribed punishment that she will suffer pain in childbearing (Gen 3:16) readers are surprised to find the opposite is true. The story appropriately begins with human procreation: Adam and Eve have sex, she becomes pregnant and gives birth to Cain and then Abel (Gen 4:1–2). Not only is nothing mentioned about her experience of pain in childbearing but she gives credit to the Creator who participates with her in giving life to another: "I have given life to a man with the LORD's help" (4:1b CEB). Terence Fretheim even allows that this act of childbearing signals an act of "human-divine cooperation" in which Eve acknowledges God's blessing of her to "increase and multiply and fill the earth" (Gen 1:28).[8] That is, it is not the act of childbearing that saves Eve but rather it is through her act of childbearing that she realizes that her covenant relationship with God is restored and blessed.

The oft-repeated phrase "this is a core belief" (3:1a; cf. 1:15; 3:1a; 4:9; 2 Tim 2:11; Titus 1:9; 3:8) that opens chapter 3 should in fact conclude chapter 2. These Pauline "sayings" are spread throughout the PE as summary

---

8. Fretheim, "Genesis," 372.

statements of Paul's interpretation of God's way of salvation. I take it that this phrase, then, looks back to Eve rather than ahead to those appointed as church leaders to underscore the idea that all women are ransomed because of Jesus. Not all will come to a knowledge of this truth through their "childbearing," even though a biological distinctive of women. While true of Eve's way of salvation, preachers must resist the temptation to make "childbearing" a trope of the domesticated female who gains or recognizes God's favor by the gifts of children and the experiences of motherhood. Some women remain single or childless for different reasons. Their stories of when they are assured of God's forgiveness or how they experience God's saving graces are plotted differently than Eve's or Paul's conversion experience on the Damascus Road (1:12–16; cf. Acts 9:1–9). Nonetheless, both Eve and Paul represent us all in that "while we were still sinners, Christ died for us all" (Rom 5:8b; cf. 1 Tim 2:5–6).

The awkward shift of subject from a particular woman ("she," 2:15a) to women in general ("they continue . . . with prudence," 2:15b) marks the conclusion of Paul's instructions regarding the public manners of certain Christian women (or wives) that ends as it begins, with an appeal for "prudence" (*sōphrosynē*, 2:9, 15b). The rhetorical effect of this "envelope" underscores the importance of this virtue as the subtext of the entire passage. Whenever the most prominent social virtue most commonly recognized in any cultural setting characterizes the public practices of a congregation's leading women, it has the persuasive power to evoke within other woman their recognition of the gospel's truth. This is the salient effect of personal testimony in public life: good manners lend integrity to the gospel's truth claims. By such testimony, women "likewise" come to know that God desires to save them from the self-destructive results of deception and sin and to transform them into persons known for their virtue—"faith and love and holiness." We take it that this would have been a radical idea in a male-centered world.

In fact, Paul contends in Romans that *every* believer is liberated from their deception and sin because of God's salvation-recreating grace (cf. Rom 5:12—6:23). For Ephesian women in particular to live "with prudence," then, is completely in character of their regeneration—their dress, their good works, their attentive learning embody the effects of God's saving grace in a person's life. Eve is an exemplar of this for every woman. If viewed from this more positive angle, Paul's interest in the pair of pedagogical contrasts drawn in 2:11–12—learning but not teaching, submitting but not leading—shifts the reader toward a more fruitful outcome, different than the experiences of some extraordinary Christian women who have been silenced by the imprudent application of this passage.

Preaching 1 Timothy 2

Sermon big idea

The key to preaching 1 Timothy 2 is to integrate its various bits into a coherent whole. The temptation is to detach any one of these bits—each of which has a history of contested interpretation—from the others and so lose sight of Paul's compass for orderly worship. Paul's target is God: prayers to God according to God's interest; confession of our faith in God who alone rescues us from death because of Christ; and social manners that embody God's interest in saving everybody.

Sermon sketch

Three more soundbites provide the key points of a sermon or lesson that unpacks a Pauline idea of "orderly worship"—that is, worship that properly centers a congregation on the things of God in a posture of thanksgiving and repentance.

1. *"First of all, I request that prayers be offered for everybody, even for kings" (2:1–2).* This is a soundbite about our allegiances. The contentious nature of today's politics and religious affiliations that characterize the social world in which we now live testify to divided loyalties. Peace is difficult to find. One group honors the persona and work of those civic leaders who rule over us while another group demonizes the persona and discredits the work of those same leaders. To the first recipients of 1 Timothy there could hardly be a more different figure of worship and adoration than "the king." Yet, Paul begins "first of all" to pray for all people, including "the king." According to this instruction, the community should not disorder their worship of God by following a politicized liturgy that either supports or subverts those who rule over us; we should rather pray to God "for kings" (*hyper basileōn*).

The pastor-teacher should first make clear that the subtext of this soundbite presumes the existence of a God whose worship admits to and demands our undivided attention. On this theological foundation, a sermon should develop God's response to a congregation's petitions "for kings" based on this passage. The *hina* clause states the purpose is to lead a "calm life." Hardly a trope for a domesticated or colonized life in which the king's rule of law is obeyed without question, this idea rather calls attention to the church's practice of retreating to "quiet" places for uninterrupted seasons of silent meditation and contemplative prayer long considered a necessary spiritual discipline of the mature believer. Jesus often did so to ready himself for the demands and difficulties of his messianic ministry. Praying to God "for kings" is not only an act of good citizenship, following the biblical example of the prophet Daniel, but also an act that embodies a Christian confession in the singular authority of God over "all humanity," including their rulers. More importantly, the congregation's prayers offered to "God our Savior" should agree with the Savior's intentions: prayers for kings petition God "the eternal King" (1:17) that their earthly kings will courageously come to a knowledge of the truth and so be saved from falsehood and any decision that is contrary to God's will.

2. *"God desires to save everybody and for them to come to a knowledge of the truth" (2:4)*. A very large element in the catechesis of any congregation is to press the point that good theology matters. Preaching should include helping congregations "come to a knowledge of the truth." Different faith traditions sponsor different theological grammars, all of which are grounded in the church's apostolic witness given partial expression by the theological summary in this passage. The second point of this sketched sermon provides a creed-like summary of the truth that targets our prayers for everyone as well as the holy ends of every practice that orders a congregation's worship of God.

The tension between the divine "one" and the human "all" is both strange and striking and should be explored (see exegetical notes). It seems strange because this confession reverses what is the norm of today's social media that pits many different self-centered individuals (the "one") against everything and everyone else, including God (the "all"). Truth, rather, centers us on "one" God whose grace is offered to "all" people. Salvation from the multifaced evils that we encounter in our daily lives has a single source, a single means to a single end because it is authored and sustained by one God. While conflict has always been provoked by this radical singularity and the exclusive nature of Christian belief in one God, one salvation, one baptism, the repetition of "all" in this Pauline formulation of truth is profoundly inclusive. In fact, the desires of one God, the atoning ransom of one particular Jewish man, whom God appointed as messianic mediator in the salvation of all, and the providential outworking of its redemptive effect in human relationships are all components of "the truth" that is the leading edge of a congregation's catechesis. Knowing the implications and applications of each of these components is critical in forming a fearless and relevant discipleship for today's broken world that is as hard as nails for Christ's sake.

3. *"This is a core belief" (3:1a).* Our prayers and confessions of faith in one God are principal practices of a congregation's worship of God. The holy end of worship is the salvation of everyone, which is the desire of the God we worship. The practice of an orderly—or what Paul might call "healthy"—worship seeks to concentrate a congregation's attention on God and upon God's way of salvation. The prayers, the hymns of praise, the confessions of faith, the offerings of our gifts, the reading aloud of scripture, and the sermon help bring to focus the truth about a God who desires to save everyone, including those we least like or whose politics and lifestyle are opposite our own. The biblical idea of salvation maintains this uneasy dance between a singular absolute—one God, one Messiah, one salvation, at God's timing—and an all-inclusive everyone, who are beneficiaries of this act that climaxes the divine economy of grace.

The coming to converting knowledge of the gospel's surprising and radical claim of what is truly true is signaled by the last catchphrase of this chapter, which is wrongly placed by later editors when copying manuscripts of 1 Timothy to open the next chapter of instruction about selecting church leadership: "You can trust this saying." This distinctive formula for Pauline summaries of God's salvation in the PE invites us to look back at the exemplary example of Eve who comes to a knowledge of the truth of her restored relationship with God when giving birth to her children (2:13–15a). Her story is everyone's story. In this cultural setting, however, contextualized by the ancient social world of Roman Ephesus in which Paul's instructions are earthed and first applied, the salvation of women equal in requirement and effect to the salvation of men would have been an extraordinary claim. God's salvation of Eve makes an even deeper impression of the inclusivity of God's way of salvation. Preachers could retell Eve's story by casting contemporary examples of those our own social worlds might think unworthy of divine grace.

But these are instructions that target a certain group of Christian women who are well known and have influence in their community. They have financial means and social standing that attract attention, especially of other women. Their allegiance to and worship of one God was embodied in their social manners. Paul lists virtues that characterize the ideal woman of his day; preachers should contemporize these virtues for our own day. What are people admired for today? What manner of life attracts attention today? Professional competence? Honesty and empathy? A reputation for good works and generous giving? We embody God's glorious gospel by what we do and say. The salvation of those who see what we do in the workplace or neighborhood and hear what we say in public or on social media depends upon it.

A passing note that good preachers might smuggle into their expositions of this text. The biblical idea of "salvation" is multifaceted: a loving, grace-giving God saves us from a variety of bad news—sin and death, the evil twins, but also physical harm or even from foolish choices. The petition "to deliver us from evil" is as expansive in scope as evil is resident in creation in a variety of spiritual and material forms. God our Savior is also God our Creator; God's economy of salvation extends to all of creation, all that is, seen and unseen.

Chapter 3

THE CHARACTER AND CAST OF CONGREGATIONAL LEADERSHIP

Exegetical Notes on 1 Timothy 3–4

THE NEXT SET OF Paul's instructions to Timothy, spread across 1 Timothy 3–4, profiles the spiritual leaders of God's household and their practices in managing and nurturing a community of believers, especially when dealing with various sorts of controversies and conflict. Paul concentrates first of all on those who lead this holy household. Priority is granted to those qualified to give oversight to this household, evinced by a résumé that includes evidence of a well-managed family household (3:4–5), a reputation for good manners (3:2–3), maturity of faith (3:6), and grace-filled rapport with non-believers (3:7). Each of these elements is noted by personal virtues that enable those competencies required of an effective leader able to shepherd the congregation, especially through conflict, and safeguard the apostle's gospel into the next generation of believers. In a second pericope (3:8–13), Paul turns to the household's "servant staff." The catalog of virtues includes characteristics of an ideal household servant (3:8, 12–13) whose faithfulness is tested and found blameless (3:9–10). Their spouses must be similarly qualified to serve others as well (3:11), since caring for members of the household is their principal responsibility.

Paul then clarifies Timothy's pivotal pastoral role in forming Christian congregations as the apostle's delegated substitute, again by using familiar household metaphors: Timothy is the "pillar and foundation of the truth within the household of God" (3:15b). The formulation of this foundational "truth" is expressed by the elegant Christological creed (3:16), which is the linchpin between Timothy's description as the household's truth-provider in contrast to opposing teachers whose "doctrines of demons" pose a threat to believers (4:1–5). In this way, "church of the living God" (3:15c) is secured by the truth of the gospel (3:16).

After an interlude that sounds an apocalyptic warning about apostate interlopers, Paul returns to more practical instructions that present a "professional development plan" for his successor. Having already encouraged Timothy to ground his ministry in "good doctrine" (4:6–7a), Paul turns now to portray the sort of person who can effectively pastor those under his care. The overarching exhortation regarding the ultimate value of a holy life (4:7b–8) is underwritten by a canonical saying that clarifies its eschatological benefit (4:9–10, cf. 15–16). The pattern of holiness commended by Paul includes both personal virtues (4:12) and vocational practices (4:13–14). Timothy is to live in a holy manner that is observed by all (4:15) so that the community may learn by his example of faithfulness what is necessary for salvation (4:16).

Although undeveloped in 1 Timothy, Paul's passing comments about the ministry of a congregation's leaders (4:14; 5:17ff.) suggest they collectively are important custodians of the truth (3:15) and indispensable agents in maintaining the spiritual health of believers. They provide leadership for those who meet together in Christian congregations for worship and instruction, good works and social fellowship. Considering the Pauline witness as a whole, some may puzzle over a biblical conception of Christian leadership that retrieves its exegetical goods only from this passage and not also from the more charismatic "body of Christ" used elsewhere in Paul's correspondence (e.g., Romans, 1 Corinthians, Ephesians). The two conceptions of the politics of a congregation are not opposite but complementary and even self-correcting. Should the more hierarchical model of managing a congregation's life become so institutionalized as to miss or even dismiss the contribution of those without ecclesial office but with spiritual charisms to offer the congregation, we would do well to hear Paul's witness to an otherwise divided Corinthian congregation about the design of a Spirit-ordered economy found in 1 Corinthians 12–14.

According to the PE, the "living God" is *paterfamilias* of a sacred household (cf. 3:15) and the political shape of this theological conception draws naturally upon the experience of middle-class households in urban centers of the Mediterranean world (cf. 1:4–5; 5:1—6:2; 2 Tim 2:20–21; Titus 1:5; 2:1–10).[1] Those charged with caring for the family household, from its administrator to its servant staff, had particular responsibilities to perform and social conventions to observe. As is true today, the progress of Roman society depended upon maintaining the stability of its various households, civil and familial. While the outlook and aim of those who lead God's household aspires to holy ends, the daily operations of any household require effective administrators and a competent servant-staff. Paul's instructions regarding the political organization of congregations is roughly analogous to its social and political practices—another example of missionary Paul's willingness to accommodate the outworking of Christian faith to those places where people actually live (cf. 1 Cor 9:19–23).

Given the centrality of the household motif in the PE, the terms Paul uses do not refer to established church offices of a highly organized episcopacy (e.g., bishops, deacons) but rather are better understood as metaphors of those practices and roles performed by administrators or servants of middle-class Roman "households." His instructions have added currency even for congregants who routinely met for worship and fellowship in a family's home (cf. Acts 16:40; 20:7–12). His subsequent references to elderly men (5:1) and actual servants (6:1–2) create a purposeful ambivalence between sacred/transcendent and secular/historical households, which forms the impression that spiritual leadership is rooted in a realistic understanding of Paul's social world where appointment of virtuous persons to care and lead its institutions was thought crucial to the wellbeing of the public square.

1. *The overseer must be blameless (3:1–7).* The word typically translated "overseer" (3:1b; *episkopē*) refers to one who manages the business of a household (Luke 19:44; Acts 1:20; 1 Pet 2:12). Its use in Acts 1:20 suggests such a person is prompted by God's calling rather than by self-promotion and its repeated use in the PE (1 Tim 3:2; 4:14; Titus 1:7) commends them as those called to care for a congregation's spiritual and social wellbeing by managing the mundane nuts-and-bolts of daily routines. In this sense, the virtues listed profile a manner of leadership that works behind the scenes for the common good of the household of God.

The run-on sentence (3:2–5) is structured to introduce "blameless" (*anepilēmptos*) as the virtue of principal importance. It provides cover for the entire catalog of sixteen characteristics that follow, nine positive and seven

---

1. See Towner, *1–2 Timothy and Titus.*

negative. In this sense, these virtues register a well-rounded public "impression" of one's moral blamelessness. The "blameless" person is well-known in Hellenistic moral philosophy, especially for their concern for cultivating the respect of outsiders. The social virtues listed taken as a whole profile a person with competence in political relationships of all kinds.

Consistent with 1 Timothy's use of household as its primary metaphor of the church, marital fidelity and well-behaved children are listed as the marks of the excellent administrator. However, in the context of the Pauline canon where the believer who is unequivocally committed to God is celebrated (see 5:9–10; cf. 1 Cor 7), the phrase "husband of one wife" might be understood more rigidly as the husband of *only* one wife. As a signature of faithful commitment to God, the administrator of a Pauline congregation may need to pledge to remain a widower in single-minded service of God's church should his wife die (cf. 1 Cor 7). I have noticed in the church's current struggle over same-sex marriage the relaxation of rules over divorced clergy, divorces that are sometimes the result of sexual improprieties. Jesus is clear about his objection to divorce, following the prophetic word of Israel's scripture; the church that confesses him as Lord, however, is not as attentive to his instruction about divorce as they are in their judgments about the sex of marriage partners.

The objection may be raised that this phrase presumes the congregation's exclusively male oversight. But later Paul stipulates the "truly needy" widow is "the wife of one man" (5:9) who qualifies for congregational support for the leading role she performs within the household. In this case, gender is not the relevant criterion of leadership but rather fidelity to God and to God's church is. By simple inference, the same is true here: that is, the virtue of "one spouse" notes compliance to the social norm of faithfulness to the household rather than to gender exclusivity.[2]

2. *Servants likewise must hold to the mystery of the faith with clear conscience (3:8–13).* The term often translated as "deacon" (*diakonos*; 3:8) belongs to a word-family (*diakonia/diakoneō*) that has wide currency in the Pauline corpus and generally conveys the disciple with a task-oriented vocation, especially noteworthy of its repetition in 2 Corinthians (see 2 Cor 3:3, 6; 5:18; 8:19–20; 11:23). The use of *diakonos* here, however, is metaphorical of household "servants" who collectively and faithfully serve God's household rather than of those appointed to the ecclesial office of "deacon." Perhaps for this reason, he says that this servant-staff must "hold

---

2. Bassler, *1 Timothy, 2 Timothy, Titus*, 66.

to the mystery of the faith with a clear conscience" (3:9)—a religious practice that distinguishes servant from household administrator. The servant must confess the "mystery of godliness" defined by creedal formula of 3:16 (cf. Eph 1:9; 3:4), since to do so insures the fitness of their work within the community. According to Hellenistic religious mores, beliefs linked to a "mystery" implied the use of magical formulae or esoteric teachings, or to an initiation ritual known only to the membership. But in Pauline teaching, the "mystery of faith" is a public statement of what is believed, which marks out the confessing community as a people belonging to Christ. In this sense, then, the servant's primary responsibility within the household is to embody in service to others what is confessed to be true about Christ as God's servant (cf. Rom 15:8; Phil 2:7).

The structure of the catalogue, then, lists four virtues that cultivate the conduct of the faithful servant's tasks within the household (3:8): "honorable, so not duplicitous, nor a drunk, or greedy." The subsequent adjective (*anegklētos*, 3:10) differs from the earlier word, *anepilēmptos*, used of the competent administrator (3:2) because of its use as a legal term for innocence (cf. Acts 23:29; 25:16). The virtues listed of the servant reflect a resistance to temptations that get people into trouble with the law and here adapted to the household's servant-staff attentive to the spiritual formation of believers. Their ability to do so depends upon forming an honorable character. (Perhaps for this reason Timothy himself is called a "good *diakonos* of Christ Jesus" in 4:6.)

An exegetical problem facing the preacher is how to understand *gynaikas hōsautōs semnas*, literally, "Likewise, women must be proper . . ." (3:11). Because the phrase is sandwiched between two halves of a virtue list, the reader reasonably assumes some connection between these women and those who constitute the diaconate of servant-elders. What remains unclear is the nature of their relationship, whether vocational (a discrete class of female servants) or marital (wives of servant-elders). Grammar alone does not settle the exegete's decision. The concluding phrase "faithful in all things" (3:11) would seem to repeat in other words Paul's evident point: the servant's principal role within the congregation is to cultivate "faithfulness in all things" and faith is most effectively formed within households led by a faithful couple, male and female (so 3:12–13).

3. *You should conduct yourself as pillar and foundation of the truth (3:14–16).* This passage seeks to clarify the role of the congregation's pastor in functional terms (rather than, say, by gender or social class). Timothy's

role is now reimagined as the house's "pillar and foundation" (3:15); his role is to uphold "the truth" of the living God in a manner that dispels the teaching of those who "adhere to deceptive spirits and doctrines of demons" (4:1). Paul's passing mention of a personal visit (3:14) lies well beyond the routines of polite discourse. In Pauline letters, references to scheduled visits are "apostolic" house calls laden with official importance. Most obvious is that Paul recognizes his personal absence from the congregation that he has delegated Timothy to pastor. Letters become suitable substitutes for Paul's apostolic presence. The instructions given in these letters are roughly what Paul would give were he there in person.

Especially crucial is defining the relationship between Timothy's delegated authority and the congregation he now shepherds. Yet another household metaphor is used: Timothy is the house's "pillar (*stylos*) and foundation (*hedraioma*) of the truth" (3:15a).[3] Rather than the architecture images of the pagan temples, "pillar and foundation" are apt metaphors of Timothy's role as guardian of the truth—a role analogous to Moses within Israel (cf. Num 12:6–8; Deut 23:2–4; 31:30). The placement of the Christological confession here (3:16) makes perfect sense if Timothy's Moses-like role is to safeguard and transmit the truth about Christ to others. Its idiom nicely recalls and elaborates Christ's role as the mediator of God's promised salvation (see 2:4–6) to clarify that the truth Timothy is delegated to uphold is the same truth that Paul proclaims to non-Jews "in faith and truth" (2:7).

Paul often adorns his letters with confessions of faith (e.g., Rom 1:3–4; 16:25–27; 1 Cor 15:3–7; Phil 2:6–11; Col 1:15–20), although rarely as robust as this one. In most cases, a confession or hymn adds a reminder to their recipients of beliefs already owned but that need to be practiced. The confession's design and placement here underscores its particular importance for Timothy as pastor of this Ephesian "congregation of the living God." The six parallel lines fashioned three pairs that make three succinct claims about the risen Jesus cast in spatial rather than temporal images. Each pair envisages a dynamic interplay between heaven and earth, between the "mystery" that angels have witnessed and the professed beliefs of the church based upon what the apostles have witnessed of the risen Christ (cf. 3:9). Two congregations, heavenly and earthly, each confirming the truth of the other (cf. Eph 3:10). It is this agreed upon truth

---

3. See Johnson, *The First and Second Letters to Timothy*, 231–32, for explanation why Timothy and not "the church of the living God" is the delayed subject of this phrase.

that envelops the cosmos, heaven and earth, all that is, seen and unseen, that Timothy is charged to uphold (3:14).

(a) He was revealed in flesh and confirmed by Spirit. The first couplet introduces the church's most critical belief about Jesus. This affirmation is of a flesh-and-blood Jesus; his public life is nothing other than the presentation of God's redemptive purpose within history (cf. 2:5–6). The heavenly complement of this belief is that Jesus' messianic mission is confirmed by the Spirit at his resurrection (cf. Rom 1:4; Acts 2:36). The odd use of verb *dikaioun* here, which I have translated "confirmed," is similar to Paul's use of this same verb in 1 Cor 6:11 in reference to the authenticating witness of "the Spirit of our God." Accordingly, we take it that the first line refers to the whole of Jesus' public mission and not just his post-Easter visitations, which is then validated as messianic by the Spirit who mediated God's power in raising him back to life according to Pauline teaching.

(b) Seen by angels and proclaimed among the nations. The second couplet reverses the spatial interplay by beginning with a belief about the witness of angels. My translation of *angeloi* as heavenly "angels" (rather than as human "messengers") preserves the heaven-earth interplay of the creed. But why an interest in an angelic line of sight to the risen Jesus? There is preserved in the Pauline canon a happy note sounded that an angelic host welcomes the risen Son of God Messiah back into its heavenly embrace (Phil 2:9–11; cf. Rev 12:5–12); and we suspect the creed links the first two parallelisms by maintaining the resurrection subtext of the previous line. That is, this belief affirms the gospel's witness to the angelic pronouncement of the Lord's resurrection (cf. Matt 28:5–7), whose confirmation is assumed by the apostolic proclamation of the risen Jesus among the nations (cf. Matt 28:16–20).

(c) Believed worldwide and exalted in glory. This final couplet commends what Paul has already professed: God our Savior desires the salvation of everyone (so 2:3–6), a redemptive vision that shapes the prospects of those who believe in Christ, even as it is already and demonstrably realized in the heavenly exaltation of their risen Lord (cf. Phil 2:5–11). While linking together the second line of the preceding parallelism ("proclaimed among the nations") and the first line of this one ("believed worldwide") makes perfect sense, the logical connection of this earth-heaven interplay is not immediately clear. I doubt the idea of the doxology's final line is predicated on a prior reading of Luke, as some scholars suggest, reading this as a nod to the Lord's ascension as the ultimate proof of his resurrection

(so Luke 24:51–54; Acts 1:3–10). The accent is Pauline and expresses Jesus' heavenly exaltation as creation's Lord and thus the utter logic of the church's trust in him and proclamation of him in the world.

4. *In the latter times, some will abandon the faith and adhere to doctrines of demons (4:1–7a).* Although most commentators argue that 4:1 marks a new unit of instruction, what follows is better understood as a contrast between Timothy's role as the "pillar and foundation of the truth" (3:15) and those who seek to subvert this truth with "doctrine of demons" (4:1). Not only does this contrast echo Paul's opening reference to those promoting "divergent doctrine" (1:3) but his invective trades on the tradition of Jesus' apocalypse (cf. Matt 24; par. Mark 13; Luke 21) that predicts the arrival of false prophets in the latter times who seek to subvert Israel's preparation for its Messiah. The powerful trope "doctrines of demons" recasts the earlier expression "divergent doctrine" (1:3) in terms of a creation-denying asceticism that evidently disregards marriage and certain foods as the good creations of a benevolent Creator (4:3–4).

Paul's correction of this anti-creational falsehood appears to follow naturally from the letter's use of "household" as metaphorical of the Christian congregation. In this regard, the quality of a covenant-keeping marriage as a credential of spiritual leadership is of a piece with this household metaphor. Any opposition to marriage or to certain foods (think hospitality), especially if received with thankful responses to the Creator's common grace, may signal teaching that is subversive not only to the sacred household's covenant with God but also to its mission in the world.

The thankful reception of material creatures such as good food or healthy social conventions, such as a covenant-keeping marriage, is sanctified for holy outcomes by the church through "God's word and prayer (of thanksgiving)" (4:4–5). In this compositional setting the consecrating agent is not the holy Spirit but the holy household. Even these mundane activities—eating good food around a table with one's extended family and friends—carry religious importance for believers, especially when contrasted with non-Christian "households" whose use of food (or not) during religious rituals framed a different natural theology than for Christians. In continuity with Jewish tradition, table fellowship is consecrated by prayers of thanksgiving that recall the biblical story of creation in which "God's word" brings forth a creation (cf. Gen 1:31) in which food (cf. Gen 1:29–30) and marriage (cf. Gen 1:28) are given strategic roles that serve the Creator's way of stewarding the world.

The subsequent conditional of 4:6–7a continues from Paul's correction of a creation-denying Christianity rather than introducing the personal charge that follows in 4:7b–16. *Tauta* ("these things") is frequently used in this letter (3:14; 4:6, 11, 15; 5:7, 21; 6:2, 11), but often without clear indication of its referent. In this use, a case could be made that *tauta* ("these things") anticipates what comes next, and in particular the canonical saying found in 4:10. However, we think it more plainly concludes the implied contrast between those teachers who seek to influence a sacred household with "doctrines of demons" and Timothy whose instruction follows the "healthy doctrine" of the Pauline legacy apropos to his vocation as the household's "pillar and foundation of the truth" (3:15). In fact, the characterization of those who fall for conspiracy theories or fake news instead of the truth as "silly" (4:7a, *graōdēs*) is a familiar trope of ancient philosophy in reference to any who substitute household remedies for science-based solutions to the ills of the day.

5. *Train yourself for godliness (4:7b–16).* The final pericope of this passage (4:7b–16) opens with the familiar typology of well-trained athletes who "train" themselves to meet targeted standards of success for "holy living" (4:7b; cf. 2 Tim 2:5). The verb "to train" (*gymnazō*, 4:7b; cf. 2 Tim 2:5) is the root from which "gym" derives as a place where the habits of a good athlete are formed. Paul, of course, is interested that Timothy use spiritual disciplines to cultivate the habits of a good pastor whose holy end is the securing of his and his congregation's future with God (4:16).

"Godliness" translates *eusebeia*, which is the most distinctive catchword for Christian existence in the PE; it is the holy end of the consistent practice of spiritual disciplines—not only worship practices already mentioned (1 Tim 2) but also scripture reading and its public hearing (4:13) as well as the practice of spiritual gifts (4:14). Paul uses *eusebeia* to characterize both the faithful congregation (2:2) and its spiritual leaders (6:3, 5–6, 11), likely trading on a well-known belief in antiquity that religious as well as social manners carry great weight in the public square. While knowing the public's high regard of earnest piety in his world, Paul also understands that the holy life heralds the coming age (4:8).

The significance of this connection between present piety and its realization in the future of God's salvation sounded by 4:8 is underwritten by repetition of the catchphrase "this teaching is a core belief" in 4:9 (cf. 1:15; 3:1a). Most commentators agree that the repetition of this phrase across the PE together summarize a Pauline way of salvation. In fact, the use of the saying here makes even better sense of Paul's concluding concern that Timothy "will save both yourself and your auditors" (4:16b). Perhaps no other PE text more clearly connects the expectation of future salvation with the present performance of one's sacred calling than this one. Sharply put, should Timothy neglect "the spiritual gift in you" (4:14), which includes the practices of a holy life (4:12, 15) and the Bible practices delegated to him (4:13, 16a), he would also neglect a "hope set on the living God" and the personal cost of doing so would be eternal.

The cultivation of godliness into a spiritual habit involves "hard work and struggle" (cf. 4:10). The pairing of "work and struggle" is frequently found in his letters to characterize Paul's missionary labor (cf. Rom 16:6, 12; 1 Cor 16:16; 1 Thess 5:12; Col 1:29). The "work and struggle" of pastoral ministry, analogous to the hard work required of physical discipline, is endured by its promissory note: the victory of salvation in this life and for the life to come.

Such a definition, of course, is predicated on one's belief in a particular kind of God: "the living God who is the Savior of all people" (4:10b; cf. 2:3–4). The combination of "living God" and "Savior" is a core Pauline belief that God enlivens "especially those who believe" as the promissory note for the life to come. Even though the universal reach of God's benefaction to "all people" continues an important theme of this letter (see 2:3–4; cf. 4:4), the use of the superlative "especially" (*mala*) restricts the *present* experience of God's promised salvation to those who have believed "the teachings of the faith" (4:6). Towner rightly concludes "there is no division here based on limited and unlimited atonement, and no need to posit two shades of meaning for the term 'Savior.'"[4] The plain sense of this core belief is that God has offered salvation to everyone but not everyone has embraced it, since divine grace does not coerce an unwilling acceptance of the gospel.

Timothy's "hard work and struggle" is in part due to his youth or inexperience, indicated by Paul's cautionary exhortation: "let no one look down on your youthfulness" (4:12a; cf. 1 Cor 16:10–11). The Roman world considered apprenticeship and field experience to be requirements of mature instruction. Paul sets out the terms of such instruction in a series of five sharply worded instructions that transcend age and job experience (4:12): (1) Practice your public speaking and social manners by instantiating in speech and life the virtues of "faith, love, and purity" (probably sexual purity; cf. 5:11–15), a triad that is the *conditio sine qua non* of

---

4. Towner, *1–2 Timothy and Titus*, 312.

effective ministry. (2) Practice scripture (4:13). The presumption here is that scripture is read aloud in public to illiterate audiences. Nonetheless, the usefulness of scripture in catechesis and pastoral exhortation is a typical formulation of Paul's (and Timothy's) Jewish sensibilities (see 2 Tim 3:16). (3) Practice the spiritual gift given you and your ordination by prophetic word and the gesture of the church's elders that recognizes your authority and fitness for congregational ministry (4:14; cf. 2 Tim 1:3; Num 27:18–23; Deut 34:9; Acts 13:1–3). (4) Be absorbed and keep practicing these things (4:15). In his famous essay "On Progress in Virtue," Plutarch extols the virtue of the person who stands up under his own scrutiny rather than is disdainful of himself as an incompetent "witness" (81a), which may help one appreciate Paul's concluding charge for Timothy to "pay close attention to yourself and to your teaching" (4:16a). (5) This concluding reminder to pay close attention to how you live and what you say is variously understood. In what sense should Timothy take responsibility for his and his congregation's salvation? The necessity of human agency in bringing to realization the promises of Gods' salvation agrees with Pauline teaching, which stipulates believers are responsible to "work out" (*katergozomai*) their salvation by God's grace and with the fellowship of believers in Christ (cf. Phil 2:12–13; 2 Tim 4:1–7). He calls believers to self-examination (e.g., 2 Cor 13:5; 1 Cor 11:27–32) along with making clear the consequence of failing to pass the test, which extends even to the apostle (so 1 Cor 9:27). Moreover, the covenant-keeping shape of a community's salvation forces a distinction between the divine source of humanity's salvation and its future realization, which is based upon works (cf. Rom 2:6–11; 2 Cor 5:10). Paul's exhortation to Timothy assumes that it is also human performance that complements divine grace that brings the living God's redemptive plan and so "our hope" to realization (4:10; cf. 1 Cor 10:32–33; 9:22). What is distinctive and perhaps confusing about this text is that the pastor cooperates with God's saving grace by engaging in ordained practices (4:14). This more vocational (rather than moral or religious) formulation of human agency is an important elaboration of Pauline soteriology and sets the stage for 2 Timothy, where this idea is given rich texture, especially by the worship practices and holy persona of Paul's faithful successor whose responsibility is to safeguard and transmit the memory and message of his apostolate.

Preaching 1 Timothy 3–4

Sermon big idea

Any single sermon whose text encompasses these two chapters will be difficult to stage-manage: these are chapters with many moving parts! But I think they hang together around the topic of *leadership* and a sermon should seek to explore how they do so. What is a biblical understanding of a good leader? Perhaps in response to well publicized stories of the moral failure of Christian leaders, the theme of leadership has become more important in a world that measures institutional effectiveness by the character of those who lead them. The moral failure of the one often leads to the religious or financial failure of the other. There is hardly another portion of scripture that speaks into this contemporary issue more powerfully than Paul's Pastoral Letters.

Sermon sketch

A three-point sermon or series of lectures/class discussions founded on these two chapters may develop the following sayings:

1. *Effective leaders must be well thought of by those outside the faith (3:1b–13).* The key idea to develop (see exegetical notes) concerns Paul's emphasis on *personal virtue*—what sort of person you are—rather than on other features of a potential leader's résumé, features that often control the search for one "who is wise and understanding among us" (Jas 3:13). Whether congregations or universities, the search often privileges the education or experiences of candidates for leadership rather than the qualities of their "blameless" character. The first sermonic point or class discussion might focus on these qualities, perhaps contemporizing Paul's catalogue in an idiom that connects with today's audience. Since "household" is the central typology used in this material, it may be worthwhile to talk—if only in passing—about the breakdown of family households in our culture because of parental inattentiveness or neglect, unchecked use of social media, hypercritical and often dismissive treatment of other members of a particular "household" (family, work, church, civic).

2. *Effective leaders should conduct themselves well in God's household because it is the church of the living God (3:14–16).* The second point is especially relevant when speaking of spiritual leadership within a Christian

or church-related congregation. The issue here (see notes) is Timothy's role as caretaker of his congregation's theological health. Effective leaders take responsibility for "the truth." While Paul includes an early Christian creed in his instructions (3:16) and exhorts Timothy to become its "bulwark" (3:15), today's clergy may want to introduce and instruct a congregation in their own confession. Pastors should think of their sermons as "catechesis"—instruction that initiates a congregation in the faith of their tradition. I have done the same in my "Introduction to the Bible" classes at a church-related university whose life is ordered by a "statement of faith." In many ways, the learning outcomes we seek in our religion classes is to nurture a particular understanding of "the truth," whether or not our students finally decide to own it as their own. Faculty are convinced that such instruction forms character that embodies truth as a way of life.

3. *Effective leaders pay close attention to how they live and what they say because by doing so they will save themselves and those who listen to them (4:1–16).* The final point is less abstract and concerns how leaders live and act, especially as they lead Christian organizations or bear witness to their Christian faith as leaders of their various "households," whether work-related or as members of civic groups. Student leaders may take special note of Paul's instructions to Timothy. Follow my exegetical notes as you exposit or work through these various exhortations. I have not found much is needed to translate the apostle's ancient advice for today. The idea of "salvation" that concludes this paraenesis may be understood in as broad a way as scripture does: not only salvation from sin and death—Paul's "evil twins"—but salvation from personal loss or congregational failure as well. We hear echoes of the Proverbs throughout these chapters, which should remind us that Paul enlists here a wisdom for the good life—human relationships ordered by the Creator's intentions for a "very good" and interdependent existence (cf. Gen 1:31).

Chapter 4

BRINGING ORDER TO THE HOUSE

Exegetical Notes on 1 Timothy 5

PAUL'S NEXT INSTRUCTIONS TO Timothy codify rules of engagement that order household relationships "with complete purity" (5:1–2). In agreement with biblical tradition, attention is paid to the welfare of widows who are "truly needy" and require the congregation's financial support (5:3–10, 16) and those young and vulnerable who are easily misled. They require the support of a family household or patron to concentrate their talent and energy (5:11–16). This is true as well of those "elders" engaged in ministry who should be fairly compensated (5:17–18). But Paul is clear that this compensation is a two-way street, so that those elders accused of malpractice should be fairly judged (5:19–25). Perhaps more controversial to today's readers is Paul's advice about household slaves, who are treated within the bounds of a covenant-keeping relationship, which accords with "the Teaching" (6:1–2).

1. These instructions are similar to other household codes found in antiquity and elsewhere in this letter. Paul draws upon this tradition to arrange human relationships according to the *oikonomia theou* ("God's economy," see my exegetical notes on 1 Tim 1:4–5). Significantly, central to the political ideology of the well-run family household is its promotion as a necessary condition of competent society. Similarly, an orderly household of believers is a necessary condition for maintaining a covenant-keeping relationship with a faithful God. Moreover, congregational care for one another impresses the outsider who observes that the witness of the "blameless" widow (see

exegetical notes on 3:2) defeats the opponent's slanderous accusation (5:14). This mixture of responsible care for insiders and conscientious regard for the opinion of outsiders (5:10) is characteristic of Paul's household code, which reflects extraordinary sensitivity to people of all ages under the banner of God's desire to save everyone (cf. 1 Tim 2:3–4).

2. The repetition of "purity" (5:2, 22; cf. 4:12) in reference to young men and women indicates a core emphasis of these instructions. Most commentators think the call to purity reflects a particular threat to the congregation's reputation, probably sexual, whose likely source is the young. "With complete purity" (5:2), then, is code for chastity. Today's use of this same moral code may extend to the language games of social media. In any case, this is the subtext of Paul's subsequent instructions regarding widows: the older widows mentor the young widows who seduce a husband with sex but without thought of Christ (5:11–15). It also underlies Paul's instruction to a youthful Timothy, who should "keep (himself) pure" (5:22b) as a condition of an effective ministry. In fact, the particular application in his case is purity of discernment in administrative matters. Purity, then, is what safeguards responsible decisions, whether about marriage or management of a congregation's jurisprudence. These instructions are apropos of an ecclesial household. The repetition of *presbyteros* in reference to age (5:1) and office (4:14) implies that good interpersonal and administrative relationships within a competent congregation are maintained by mutual respect (cf. 1:5) rather than by abusive force.

3. Of primary concern for Timothy's urban congregation is "to care" (*timaō*, 5:3) for widows (5:3–16); "care" is a primary verb that controls the action of this chapter. The congregation shoulders the responsibility of caring for its most vulnerable members—the widows. This same verb is often translated "honor"; to practice care of its widows is a congregational hallmark and brings "honor" to its presence in the public square (cf. Acts 6:1–7).

Paul's instructions for widow-care are in line with the teaching of Jewish scripture: Torah demands the covenant-keeping community take special care of its widows and orphans, its most vulnerable members (Exod 22:22; Deut 14:29; cf. Zech 7:9–10). Although Roman law required that a widow would be provided for by her deceased husband's household or her own, the infrastructure of the congregation's welfare system follows scripture rather than Roman law (cf. Acts 6:1–6; 9:39; Jas 1:26–27; Luke 7:11–17). As such, the congregation's widows are divided into three groups: (1) those who are "truly needy" due to their age and lack of financial support from their extended family and whose piety is exemplary (5:3, 5–7, 9–10); (2) those who should expect the financial support of their children (5:4, 8, 16); and (3) those who are still young and should expect to remarry (5:11–15).

The practice of putting widows "on a list" (5:9) is well-known from Hellenistic literature. This registry of widows in need of the congregation's material support has less to do with keeping a public record of those worthy of support than as motivation to follow Paul's instruction of care. In this regard, among a widow's qualifications are her age and faithfulness: she is "not less than sixty years old" and "the wife of one man" (5:9; cf. 3:2), evidence of her faithful character. Paul is concerned that the congregation, whose vocation is to engage the wider culture with the gospel, is not at odds with social convention. At the same time, he is concerned that Christian widows are known for their piety (5:5) and "good works" (5:10). The catalogue of good works found in verse 10 is thematic of the Christian life in the PE (cf. 2 Tim 3:17) and characteristic of the public operations of divine grace.

Paul's admonition that he "preferred that younger widows marry" probably went against the conventions of his day: widows generally remained single, depending on the graces of their families. His instruction is grounded in a belief that marriage constrains bad behavior (5:11–13; cf. 1 Cor 7:8–9), which would "give the opponent no opportunity to slander us" at Satan's instigation (so 5:15). This is not a reflection of Paul's misogyny but of his practical concern that dependent widows can find themselves idle, with no family to care for and no need to work. This situation may open the door to temptations to sexual misconduct, particularly for the young (5:13; cf. Titus 1:11–12). Hence, Paul's preference that younger widows marry. Dependent widows were perceived as morally lax (cf. Aristotle, *Nicomachean Ethics* 1097b), although younger widows almost certainly would have carried a sexual overtone in Paul's world (5:11; cf. Dio Cassius *Roman History* 47:15.4; 53:2.4). Sexual failure by believers was a vote against the gospel in antiquity, as it remains today.

4. The chief threat to the spiritual vitality of younger widows is expressed by a compounded verb, *katastrēniasōsin*, whose meaning is very difficult to determine (5:11). The prefix *kata-*, aims the reader at practices that are "against" Christ; and then to an earlier "confession of faith" (*pistis*) these believers had made to or about him (5:12). The verbal root, *strēniaō*, denotes a strong compulsion or inclination toward some desire, in this case to get married. I have translated the verb "distracted" to convey a relational

sense: pursuit of a marital relationship at the expense of a relationship with Christ. If this is the case, then "Christ" in this passage is existentially adduced and refers to the living Christ rather than to "Christology" or a body of beliefs about Christ that are jeopardized by a different preoccupation. What is imperiled is a prior confession of faith in Christ, which must have included a vow of single-minded devotion similar to that embodied in the older widows (5:10). This concern is not unlike that expressed by Paul in 1 Corinthians 7, both in his preference that they remain unmarried to better serve the interests of Christ but also in allowing them to marry rather than to be distracted by sexual desire (1 Cor 7:8–9). Against the backdrop of this antecedent Pauline text, the subsequent and apparently contradictory instruction to marry (5:14) must be understood as the pastoral solution for the believer whose pronounced desire to find a husband now imperils her life with Christ (5:11–12).

5. The vague reference to the believer who "has widows" (*echei chēras*; 5:16) has been variously interpreted, despite the efforts of scribes who added to the text to make its intent more plain. The feminine form of "believer" is used (*pistē*), which indicates the instruction is aimed in particular at the Christian woman. Most interpreters qualify the widows as her relatives, extending the earlier injunction that families should take care of their own. In this sense, to "have widows" in the family implies a responsibility toward them. While this reading is certainly plausible and continues the letter's interest in the financial responsibility of middle-class Christian women (cf. 2:10; 6:17–19), it does not explain why this instruction is necessary since it repeats a point made earlier (by 5:8), nor why it focuses exclusively on female disciples.

Perhaps it is better to take the most common sense of "have" as to possess or own something. That is, this instruction is directed at wealthy female Christians (cf. 2:9), whose personal servants are widows for whom they are directly responsible as members of their extended household. The scope of the earlier rule is here expanded to include non-familial relationships within the household. This is consistent with Pauline paraenesis in which the traditional hierarchy of household relationships in the Jewish/Roman world are reset to embody the mutuality that exists in Christ (so Gal 3:28; Col 3:11) as a real-world microcosm of the *oikonomia theou* whose aim is love (cf. 1:4–5), especially in those social relationships where abuse is likely. It would also seem to bring balance in the subsequent instruction aimed at household slaves in 6:1–2.

Even as Paul's earlier instructions concentrate upon widows, presumably because of the community's special responsibility toward them, so too here a particular group of older men are in view: those who lead the congregation and especially those who have assumed important and sometimes difficult public roles (5:17). Leadership within middle-class households of antiquity was typically determined by gender (male) and age (elderly) and this social norm here extends to God's household—even if Paul is probably less concerned about chronological age than spiritual maturity (see 3:6; 4:12).

6. Payment of a "double honorarium" is consistent with the congregation's policy of the financial support given its older members. The formula "For the scripture says" (5:18) introduces LXX Deut 25:4, "Do not muzzle the ox that is threshing," which combined with "The worker is worthy of his wages" probably recalls instructions regulating the fair compensation of priests (cf. LXX Num 18:31). Paul uses a well-known device of rabbinical rhetoric, first appealing to scripture's lesser claim—in this case, a farm animal—to prove scripture's ultimate claim—in this case, a fair wage for the laborer of the gospel. That is, if we generally treat beasts of burden fairly, then *how much more* should we treat fairly those teaching elders who labor on God's behalf. Significantly, Jesus uses a similar wisdom when instructing his disciples for mission (see Luke 10:7). The resulting intertext between 1 Tim 5:18b and Luke 10:7b lends Christ's support to the principle of fair compensation for those who "labor in public speaking and teaching" (5:17).

The support of the congregation's teaching elders is of a piece with its support of teaching widows of a similar age, who were added to the welfare roll in part because of their "good works" (see 5:10). In this next case, their good works are "public speaking and teaching" (5:17). Not only would competence in public speaking be considered a sine qua non for effective leadership in antiquity, the distinction between the two activities regards their different audiences and intentions, the first directed toward outsiders and the second to the church. And this is hard work! The word used for "labor" is not *ergeō* as one might expect but *kopiaō*, which envisages the kind of sweaty exertion that exacts a physical toll on a daily laborer.

The antecedent use of Deut 25:4 in 1 Cor 9:9, where Paul links its current meaning with his compensation as the congregation's teacher (see 1 Cor 9:14), presents another example of the PE as hermeneutical collection (see above, pp. 5–6). Evidently, Paul had earlier been accused by some in the Corinthian congregation of not behaving as a leader should because he had refused their financial support—a problem, then, if this refusal is taken as an act of noncompliance with scripture's exhortation. By appeal to Deut 25:4, then, he agrees with those who say that he is entitled to the congregation's support because God is concerned that hardworking people are treated fairly—even more so than hardworking oxen! But on grounds that his "apostleship [is] in the Lord" (1 Cor 9:2), he declines this right to a fair wage (so 1 Cor 9:15a).

But clearly the situation has changed in 1 Timothy. Perhaps because the letter is occasioned by the apostle's departure from the congregation, the prerogatives of Paul's apostleship, including his earlier renunciation of financial support, have departed with him and are not passed on to others. Instead, his successors who "lead well" and work hard to teach his gospel to others should be fairly compensated for doing so.

7. While nothing is said about a list of elders approved for financial support (cf. 5:9), a similar attention is required of Timothy focused by the sparse warning against the hasty ordination of unfit elders (5:22). As before with the widows, Paul's instruction concerns the quality of both work and character: unrepentant sinners are unfit to lead a congregation (5:20)! In such cases Paul provides a jurisprudence to order the congregation's support of its leaders (5:17–18). Paul's instruction again trades on Torah's injunction about credible evidence (5:19; cf. Deut 19:15): no verdict is rendered when an accusation is leveled against an elder without multiple eyewitnesses (5:19). Only the credible evidence of impartial witnesses determines the guilt of an elder. The purpose of church discipline in this case is not the spiritual repair of the guilty party (as is the Lord's jurisprudence, according to Matt 18:15–17) but the loss of their spiritual authority to lead the congregation.

Reading this instruction in canonical context enables us to see that it reverberates with echoes of prophetic cross-examinations of exiled Israel before an impartial heavenly court that issues a verdict on evidence of guilt and a fair judgment of exile (and related losses). Paul's instruction, seen in this context, provides a cautionary note to Timothy not to preside over a kangaroo court. A trial before an impartial God, who fairly considers all relevant evidence (cf. LXX Sir 35:12, Rom 2:11; 1 Pet 1:17), requires the same of "the church of the living God" (3:15). To blithely ordain (lit., "lay hands upon") elders (5:22) or to neglect their moral carelessness is subversive of a congregation's perseverance (cf. 4:16).

8. The repeated exhortation "keep yourself pure" (5:22b; cf. 4:12; 5:2) is for good reason. Timothy's youth may be perceived by some in the congregation as inexperience or lack of wisdom. Perhaps even Paul views Timothy's immaturity as a liability in gaining the congregation's confidence during the sometimes tricky negotiations of a disciplinary proceeding of an accused elder. Even the "use of a little wine" would have been viewed as prescription for a "nervous stomach"; the Talmud stipulates wine as the "first among medicines" (*b. Ben Bat.*, 58b; cf. *b. Ber.* 35b).

But even a glass of wine taken to settle an upset stomach is no substitute for Timothy's fitness to discern the sinner who needs rebuke and repair from the flawed saint who needs support and pastoral encouragement. Assessing people is the truck-and-trade of Timothy's job description. Appropriately, then, the final instruction (5:24–25) is given in the third person as though axiomatic. The contrast between "good works" that are evident (*prodēlos*, 5:25) and hidden forms of inward sin (cf. 5:21) would seem to suggest that Timothy must wait upon the consequences of behavior before assessing it. What is blatantly sinful or conspicuously good is not difficult for people to measure; however, the full effect of what is hidden from public scrutiny is more difficult to discern. Rather enigmatically, Paul reminds Timothy that the consequence of what one does "cannot remain hidden from view." Perhaps it can be hidden from Timothy as their pastor, but not from the heavenly tribunal of "God, Christ Jesus and the elect angels" (5:21; cf. Heb 4:12–13).

9. Since most middle-class urban households of the Roman world included household slaves, conduct codes typically included instructions to regulate relations between slaves and their household managers: responsibilities and conduct. What is remarkable about Paul's household code is the *motive* of good conduct: slaves are to serve the household well so "the Teaching" may not be reviled (6:1) and their competence is embodied "more fully" for all to see (6:2).

For today's Christians, this passage and its vivid image of "the yoke of slavery" has made it a colonializing "text of terror." We ought not preach this passage in today's social worlds without an awareness of the history of its interpretation in worlds very different from our own. The fact that household managers are not asked to return the slaves' respect and good will has led some believers to use this text to endorse a social hierarchy that sanctions the oppression of others for God's sake; we should consider such practice blasphemous.

The pastor-teacher may well call attention to the fact that the holy end of any biblical interpretation is to form deeper love for God and one another. However, the case can also be made exegetically that most middle-class households in the Greco-Roman world included slaves and so traditional conduct codes included rules that reflected their duties. The family households from which Timothy's Ephesian congregation drew its members evidently included household slaves, who were crucial to the economy of Roman urban society. Often these slaves were well-educated and given much responsibility for maintaining the wellbeing of the family household. To bring holy order to the relationship between slaves and their Christian masters (or owner-employers) would have been an expected element of Paul's sense of the congregation's adherence to *oikonomia theou* in his day (see 1:4).

Because his sensibilities are theological more than sociological, Paul radicalizes his world's slave-master relationship in important ways. For instance, because he allows that Christian "slaves" might work for a non-believing household (6:1), he exhorts them to "care" (*timē*) for their non-Christian households in the same way members are to care for relationships within the Christian household (see use of *timē* in 5:3, 17).

Perhaps a more surprising concern is reflected by a second kind of slave-master relationship, set out in verse 2, which stands outside of a traditional household code. Similar to Paul's letter to Philemon, the implied question is this: In what ways is a slave-master (or employee-employer) relationship transformed when both are believers? Surely this passage reflects the egalitarian (and unsettling) impress of Paul's gospel (so Gal 3:28) when applied to traditionally hierarchal arrangements. The use of the intimate "brothers" (*adelphoi*) actually reverses the move found in the Epistle to Philemon, where master Philemon is pressured to resist the societal norm and to treat his former servant, Onesimus, as his "dear brother" (*adelphos agapētos*; Phlm 16). The present instruction is as shocking to the modern reader as it must have been to Timothy precisely because it is the *slave* who is asked to regard his owner as an *adelphos agapētos* in order to maintain an otherwise cultural norm that is antithetical to "the Teaching." It is not the caring master who is responsible for righting a broken relationship, even though he would be in a position of power to do so legally; rather, it is the powerless slave who takes responsibility for a ministry of reconciliation.

The chiastic shape (A-B-A') of this passage places Paul's worry about reviling Christian teaching about God (6:1b) as the centerpiece of similar instructions regarding non-believing (6:1a) and believing masters (6:2a) to underscore the pivotal importance for believers, no matter their circumstance, to uphold "the name of God and the Teaching" (*hē didaskalia*, 6:1b; cf. 1:10–11), especially in their most awkward social relationships.

10. A final cautionary note must be sounded, more hermeneutical than exegetical. The history of interpreting this biblical passage illustrates the danger of applying biblical prescriptions to every social location. The slave catechism in the antebellum church, especially in the South, which was written by wealthy Christian slave owners to justify a money-making institution, included this text for biblical justification. Preachers and teachers alike must be alert to and reject any interpretation, even if linguistically plausible, that subverts scripture's intended purpose of cultivating loving communion with a loving God and all others, even our enemies. For this reason, a literal reading of the phrase "the yoke of slavery" too easily misses the irony of Paul's injunction and is transformed into a political reason for the powerful to control the powerless. What must be pressed in any reading of this text is what stands at its center: "that the name of God and the Teaching may not be reviled." Herein lies the real purpose of this letter for every reader and every working relationship according to the *oikonomia theou* (see 1:4–5).

Preaching 1 Timothy 5

Sermon big idea

We live in unsettled times. Various causes may be charted to explain the increase of division and conflict we experience in our social worlds: in our families, in our workplaces, in the congregations where we worship, and in the schools where we teach and study. Paul's use of the family household to help Timothy imagine how to bring order to an ecclesial setting that seems always on the verge of disorder and dysfunction provides a path to help us propose ways of settling conflict and ending the chaos we routinely experience around us.

Sermon sketch

This sermon can be indexed by recent research, especially from non-profit/voluntary community associations, that examine what makes for successful, competent communities. What I find interesting (and encouraging) is the frequent use of "household" and "familial" tropes to help leaders envision a human resources department that actually works well to eliminate potential conflict and chaos. In my reading, five qualities are crucial in building effective communities: responsiveness to questions/concerns of members, promptness to meet evident problems, informed leadership, respectful exchanges between members, and the importance of follow-up protocols to see whether solutions/answers/responses are effective. I find it remarkable how these same qualities are present in Paul's instructions to Timothy. Let me suggest a three-point sermon or class discussion that applies the following wisdom sayings that envision a biblical way of bringing order to a conflicted community.

1. *Care for widows who are truly in need* (5:3). The repetition of the language of caring for one another. The Greek word *timē* is often translated "honor," "respect," or even "support" in English and these translations carry important connotations of a biblical conception of homecare. (See exegetical notes.) Among the important concerns raised by current research is how important communication is in conveying respect and care for another. This is especially important in a world in which social media is often used to bully, to badmouth, to profane, to advance an agenda or ideology without wiggle room, and so on. Social media has become a disruptive force in our culture, even though it can be used to redeem the time. This may be an occasion to speak into a congregation or classroom's use of social media in terms of it effects on relationships with others.

Need-based support of the "truly needy," socially and financially, is critically determined. By this, I mean it is not subject to political pressures or arbitrary biases but by a careful analysis of who in the congregation is "truly needy" (because of age or absence of filial support) and whose virtue and résumé of ministry are deserving of a congregation's support.

2. *Concentrate on the good works of a pure life, which are obvious to others and can't remain hidden* (5:25). Jim Wallis once remarked that the primary reason non-Christians don't become Christians is because of Christians. He was speaking not only about the sin of hypocrisy and the threat it poses to the church's witness to the gospel but also about a spiritually deflated church whose political and moral practices are no different than other nonreligious groups. The question rightly raised in such a setting is, "What difference does Christ make in the manner of one's life?" Paul's instructions to an inexperienced Timothy underscore the importance of his self-presentation to

the public as a representative of the "church of the living God" (3:15). This admonition is true of all believers. Paul's exhortation, "keep yourself pure" (5:22b), is not a kind of paranoia but a demand of ministry grounded in the experience of leaders whose public witness has been compromised by their untoward behaviors toward others. One imagines that Paul's cautionary note not to elevate someone too quickly to a position of congregational leadership recognizes that sharing "the common sins of others" (5:22a) discredits the gospel's claim for a transformative grace that changes the manner and motives of human existence.

What is extraordinary about this paraenetic unit that concerns the obligations and relations of a Christian household is the importance Paul places upon a public or embodied purity. Some varieties of Christian devotion press the importance of the inward life—changes in how we think of ourselves and others as recipients of God's saving grace. Important, yes. But in these instructions, Paul is primarily concerned about "good works that are evident" (*prodēlos*, 5:25) and that cannot remain hidden from public view for long. The same is said of bias or prejudice, which pressures inward or hidden motives that produce bad or sinful results. While making accusations without evidence is strongly warned against and public practices of purity encouraged, there is here sufficient grounds to also challenge a congregation or classroom about the danger of inward thoughts that "cannot remain hidden" and that in due time are embodied in impure works.

3. *Care for others so that God's name and Christian teaching will not be discredited* (6:1). The angle the preacher takes when approaching hard texts makes a difference in how—and even whether—they will be received by a congregation. Sometimes a text is made hard by the preacher's prophetic posture—preaching to afflict the comfortable—when a priestly approach—preaching to comfort the afflicted—is more true to the intent of the text itself. There is no more demanding passage to preach in 1 Timothy than Paul's instructions to "those under the yoke of slavery" (6:1–2). The more prophetic reading of this conduct code used to engage today's workplace practices might deplore the conditions of an underpaid working class and so criticize Paul's tolerance for a social institution that featured an enslaved class, even though a necessary socioeconomic feature of his Roman world. However, a priestly reading of this same passage might underscore the importance of an economic household's "care" for one another no matter the rank of its members. To do so might press the imperative of theologizing our workplaces—to concentrate on practices

that uphold "the name of God" in our office or with our clients—before we moralize on their inequity or poor work conditions. The balance between prophetic and priestly is difficult to maintain; however, one or the another may seem more apropos of a particular time zone and zip code.

Chapter 5

MONEY PROBLEMS AND POSSIBILITIES

Exegetical Notes on 1 Timothy 6

REPETITION OF THE LETTER'S familiar exhortation for Timothy to instruct the congregation "about these things" (6:2b; see 4:11; 1:3; 2:1; 5:1; cf. 3:14–15) cues a familiar problem: the presence of false teachers who require young Timothy's attention. The sharp contrast between true and false teachers (6:2b–10) forms with 1:3–17 the letter's *inclusio*. Paul's instructions between the letter's two bookends develop what this passage aptly summarizes: a congregation's most influential membership—its spiritual (cf. 6:3–16) and societal leaders (cf. 6:17–19)—must be shaped not only by the "healthy teachings about (*logoi*) our Lord Jesus Christ" (6:3; cf. 1:15–16; 3:16; 6:13) but by their earnest pursuit of a godliness that is guided by these canonical teachings (6:11–16; cf. 1:11–17; 2:9–16; 3:14–16; 4:11–16).

1. The translation of *logoi* as "teachings *about*" (rather than "teachings of") takes "our Lord Jesus Christ" as an objective genitive, which agrees with the plain sense of 1 Tim 3:16: Paul's core beliefs about the exalted Christ—the "mystery of the faith"—not only provides the inward motive of a godly life but also, when embodied, the hard evidence of a good leader (cf. 1 Tim 2:9). Moreover, the repeated use of "healthy" (see 1:10) again creates a link between what is taught and what John Wesley called a "vital piety" or in Pauline terms, "godliness" (*eusebius*). True to Paul's interests in his correspondence to Timothy, neither the identity nor contested beliefs of those "who teach differently" are given. His condition for compliance with his apostolic tradition is set out in a single run-on

sentence (6:3–5). The *apodosis* (6:3a) introduces the opponent as anyone who does not follow his canonical teachings about Christ; it is practically impossible for such a person to embody *eusebius* (cf. 4:7–8) as they exhibit "an unhealthy interest in contesting the meaning of words" (6:4; cf. 1:6–7). Stupid does as stupid is! Much like today's political climate, the terrible consequence of any body politic to come under the influence of a teacher interested only in trivial pursuits is a household "deprived of the truth" (6:5) without a moral compass (so 6:4–5).

2. The haunting refrain that such a teacher fakes godliness as a money-making scheme may have in mind the Lord's contrarian teachings about wealth, which is one of the most important *topoi* of discipleship. Despite the inherent dangers of wealth, monetary attitudes (6:10) and related practices (6:17–19) are among the most "evident" ways in which a community's "good works" help people envision God's transformative grace (cf. 5:25). Perhaps Paul's ironical repetition of "great profit (*porismos*)" cues God's preferential option for a spiritual bottom line grounded in "teachings about the Lord Jesus Christ" (6:3b; so also 3:9, 16). Ironical because this "great profit" is marked by the current secular ideal of "contentment" (*autarkeia*). Yet, in 2 Cor 9:8 Paul posits that *autarkeia* comes from the overflow of divine grace, which enables the congregation to give generous gifts to the poor. This concern for a practical divinity, glossed by Paul's missionary vocation, routinely compels him to reinterpret secular ideals: in this case, for the Cynic's idealization of the simple life that empties the "self" of self-sufficiency (and self-centered envy) to produce a contented life. In this sense, of course, while we take nothing of material value out of this world at death (so 6:7), the true believer can certainly bring valuables of a spiritual kind from this world into the next (see 6:19). In this sense, godliness is the way of wisdom because its profit has eternal purchase.

The gravitas of the spiritual leader's struggle is over inward affections. Paul emphasizes this point once again by poetic resonance, using a series of π-words to create an interplay between a person's desire for riches (*plouteō*) and "tripped up (*em-piptō*) into temptation (*peirasmos*) and a trap (*pagis*)." The addition of "cravings" (*epithymia*) captures this exhortation's central deception: a self-possessed craving for financial security is the means of personal contentment (cf. Jas 1:13–16).

Although the kind of "ruin and destruction" awaiting those who are trapped by their love of wealth is not specified, the image echoes other biblical texts about God's final judgment to create a terrifying intertext (e.g., 2 Pet 2–3; Matt 7:13; Phil 3:19–20; 1 Thess 5:3; 2 Thess 2:3; Rev 17:8–11). The sense of the ruination of those who advance theological falsehood for love of money is eschatological, even when their immediate success might suggest otherwise. On this basis, Paul can reasonably conclude with his Jewish inheritance that elevating money over God is the source of every kind of mischief (see Jas 4:1–2). The placement of the word "root" (*hriza*, 6:10) at the beginning of the proverb he cites—"the root of all kinds of evil is the love of money"—intensifies a practical wisdom that greed is the source of self-destruction. In canonical context, this proverb takes on an eschatological dimension: the "many pains" of those who pursue wealth at the expense of godliness are finally experienced at the final judgment of God.

The middle voice of the present participle *oregō*, "having aspired," used earlier of those who "aspire" to lead the congregation (3:1), is used here of an opposite aspiration that motivates a congregational leader interested in his own benefits rather than in the benefaction of divine grace. The reader cannot help but recall Paul's stunning conclusion to an earlier exhortation in which he bids Timothy to obey his sacred calling to save both himself and his congregation (see 4:16), presumably to save them all from this unhappy end.

3. Timothy's personal pursuit of godliness as "God's man" is marked out by memories of an exemplary Christ (6:11–12). In contrast to the unholy end of the false teacher whose avarice tempts and traps him into a manner of life that leads to eschatological "ruin and destruction" (6:9), those who follow Christ's example will also make their "good confession" before God who alone "dispenses [eternal] life" (6:13–16).

The idiom of this passage is juridical. The emphatic naming of Timothy as "God's man" recalls an important title of the OT prophet (esp. Elijah in 1–2 Kings), who is identified as God's witness to Israel, a carrier of God's word (cf. 2 Tim 3:17), and a prosecutor of God's case against Israel and the nations. Timothy's prophetic ministry as the congregation's leader is to carry God's word to God's people so that they will come to understand God's truth (cf. 1 Tim 2:4–7).

The "flee/pursue" pairing is a conventional contrast of paraenetic literature—often used, as here, with an athletic trope (6:12a)—to make clear the sort of person who offers for all to see a persuasive witness to God. Paul's catalogue of six virtues envisions the successful pursuit for God's approval (6:13) is headed by "moral rectitude" (*dikaiosynē*) and "piety" (*eusebius*), the essential habits in cultivating a manner of life that embodies a right relationship with God and neighbor. The familiar pairing of faith and love (see 1:14) combines with a final pair, patience and gentleness, to define the qualities of a covenant-keeping fitness that endures to the end (6:12b).

A metaphor from athletic contests is used to underscore the seriousness of Timothy's pursuit of this manner of life. Already Paul has warned him that his future with God depends upon faithful attention to his vocation (4:16); and now again the reward of "eternal life" is predicated upon "competing the good race of the faith" (6:12; *agōnizou ton kalon agōna tēs pisteōs*). The exhortation to "lay hold" (*epilambanō*) suggests the workout regimen of a disciplined athlete who trains hard for victory. Eternal life is not the entitlement of those God elects or those who suppose that God has already done all the heavy lifting and all that God requires is faith alone. God's gift of eternal life is offered to all but received by those who "lay hold" of God and cultivate those habits of covenant-keeping fitness.

4. The pairing of the aorist verbs "call" (passive—i.e., called by God) and "confess" (active—i.e., Timothy confesses) recalls Timothy's prior ordination when the elders commissioned him to charismatic ministry in response to prophecy (see 4:14; cf. Acts 13:1–3). Here is emphasized a past event when Timothy responded to public confirmations—in prophecy and liturgy—of his sacred call to ministry: he "confessed the good confession" (6:12; *homologēsas tēn kalēn homologian*) before a jury of church elders, the triune God who called him, and "our Lord Jesus Christ," his standard of faithfulness to God's calling (6:13; cf. v. 3). The repetition of the adjective "good" (*kalos*, 6:12) in two phrases ("good race of the faith" and "good confession before many witnesses") with related nouns frames the résumé that results in eternal life (cf. 4:16). The key exhortation to "lay hold of eternal life" (*aiōnios zōēs*) sandwiched between makes clear the direction of Timothy's quest is toward God who alone can give such life (6:13).

What Timothy had earlier confessed at his ordination, which has become the criterion of his present ministry and future status with God (see 4:14–16), coheres to the confession the Messiah made before Pilate (6:13). "Confession" literally means "same saying" (*homo-logia*) and so invites the reader to recall the gospel tradition of Christ's Roman trial before Pilate as roughly analogous to the situation and demand now facing Timothy in Roman Ephesus. Initially, one realizes that this tradition is part of the body of "teachings about our Lord Jesus Christ" (6:3), which forms the continuing criterion that measures the content and character of a teacher's faithfulness to the sacred tradition. For Timothy to "confess the good confession," then, is to give public expression to the same kind of response Jesus made when interrogated by Pilate (cf. John 18:28–38).

The gospel's "teaching about the Lord Jesus Christ" (6:3) before Pilate may help trigger Timothy's memory of the pledge he made at his ordination (see 4:14; cf. 2 Tim 1:6–8). His personal struggle over its obligations, thematic of 2 Timothy and hinted at throughout this letter, may well envisage the same kind of conflict instantiated in Jesus that led him to the cross. Timothy's opposition to false teachers, whose confession is "deprived of the truth" (cf. 6:5), reflects this same conflict. Pilate's deeply ironical question put to the Lord, "What is truth?," is the implied question now put to Timothy, especially since a "knowledge of the truth" is God's chief desire (so 2:4) and so the central motive of Christian ministry and worship. To pledge one's allegiance to a sacred calling is to commit oneself to a costly ministry of the truth that encounters the same enemy and perhaps the same destiny as Jesus did. Paul strikingly calls Timothy's ordination "the command" (6:14) and his absolute obedience to it— "without fault or failure"—intensifies the importance of compliance, since his salvation and that of others depends upon it (so 4:16).

5. The grammar of the concluding doxology (6:15–16) is awkward and its referent is unclear, whether it refers to the majesty that accompanies Jesus' arrival as "Lord of lords, King of kings" (see Rev 19:16) or to the sovereignty of the God who alone knows its date (cf. Acts 1:6–7). Most commentators agree that its subject is God and parallels 1:17 in summarizing the core beliefs about Israel's God. While one might allow that the Lord's appearance will witness to the truth of these claims, even as it is this God to whom he testifies before Pilate, the primary focus of this passage is the contrast between Timothy and false teachers, their character and respective destinies. The impress of Paul's laudation is to underwrite the eventual triumph of those whose values and activities side with God's redemptive purpose. The unhappy future of those teachers who spread falsehoods rather than Jesus and who seek money rather than piety is made certain by the sort of God who awaits them: the transcendent authority of the one and only God guarantees a just verdict on what people have done with their lives. The catalog of divine attributes in verse 16 takes some qualities essential to human beings and reveals them to be inapplicable to the divine nature: God is not mortal (*a-thanasia*), not approachable (*a-prositos*), not visible (*hos eiden oudeis*; cf. 1:17). In the same way, God's

judgments are unlike those of human cultures; they are certain and eternal. In a world that deified its rulers (Caesar was routinely confessed as "Lord of lords") and whose gods were paraded in public as "the most powerful, the mightiest of the gods, the far-seeing master who fulfills everything"—as Homer would say of Zeus (*Ode to Zeus* 1–2)—Paul's implied claim is that sovereignty belongs only to the Creator and lordship only to Jesus Christ. This doxology registers a community's unwavering confidence in the ultimate triumph of God's way of ordering reality precisely because of the nature of God who does the ordering.

Finally, the juxtaposition of the Lord's confession before Pilate, symbolic of Rome's unholy hegemony in Palestine, and the doxology of the incomparable "Lord of lords, King of kings" are politically pregnant. Similar to Paul's earlier instruction for the community to pray for civil rulers (2:2) while believing in the singularity of God's redemption through Christ Jesus (2:3–6) and instruction through the apostle Paul (2:7), the community's theocentric faith allows no wiggle room for the prerogatives of Rome's manifest destiny. The idiom of faithful suffering the reader finds in 2 Timothy, which is the consequence of following the pattern of Pauline teaching in a public square policed by Rome, makes it impossible for us to accept the modern critical verdict of the church's wholesale domestication. At the end of the day, the conflict between the church and empire is never a seditious one; the church is a household of good citizens. Yet, no matter how compliant the church is with Roman rule or how virtuous its leadership, its core belief in one God who alone is King over all other kings, including Caesar, must be assessed (and was) as a challenge to Roman sovereignty.

6. Paul's instruction regarding wealth (see 6:3–10) not only targets the congregation's spiritual leaders, such as Timothy, but also its wealthy members who doubtless support the congregation financially but attract public attention (cf. 2:9–16). The exhortation to both is the same: those who are guided by their hope in God rather than by the sufficiency of their wealth (6:17) are rightly motivated "to be rich in good deeds" (6:18) thereby preparing for themselves a future reward (6:19).

If the Letter of James addresses spiritual problems prompted by a community's lack of wealth (esp. Jas 4:1—5:6), 1 Timothy addresses the spiritual problems of some who have wealth. In their case, the "good confession" must include the use their resources "to do good" (6:18). This instruction continues from the prior affirmation of a sovereign and transcendent God whose eschatological judgment at the appearance of the church's returning Lord either "gives life to all things" (6:13) or assigns those who substitute senseless desires for love of God to "ruin and destruction" (6:9). This haunting sense of a future judgment is reflected by the location of the rich "in the present age," the idiom of Jewish apocalypticism in which the symbols of present and coming "ages" are contrasted. Moreover, the storage of good works awaits a future whose prospect is "what is truly life" (6:19). While the Pauline belief in the consummation of God's salvation is not cast here with customary urgency or in the idiom of its imminent arrival, the future reward of faithfulness remains an important motive for a community's obedience to God.

The phrase that I translate "what is truly life" (*tēs ontōs zōēs*, 6:19b) concludes this letter's adumbration of the Christian conception of real living. The prior doxology fills out the persona of "the living God" (3:15) who gives life to all things (6:13) but "eternal life" (1:16; 4:8; 6:12) in particular to those who obey God. The ultimate proof of what is "truly life" is a life with God that endures forever.

Preaching 1 Timothy 6

Sermon big idea

Money, money, money. There is hardly a topic more consistently preached in the church and taught in the academy than money: how to get it, save it, and spend it. John Wesley taught the early Methodists, most of whom were from the working classes, that money is an "excellent gift of God for use in answering the noblest ends: it is food for the hungry, drink for the thirsty, clothes for the naked, a place for the traveler and stranger to lay their heads." For this reason, he encouraged his vast congregation of eighteenth-century England in his famous sermon "On the Use of Money" to "earn all you can, save all you can, and give all you can." He quipped, however, that while the growing middle-class members of his movement's parishes were quite good in following the first two rules, they were not as disciplined in satisfying their holy end: to give all you can to the poor.

This chapter surely addresses the dangers of wealth and how the single-minded ambition to grow one's bank account—the idolatry of wealth—is at the root of a people's disaffection with God, God's purposes, and God's holy ends. Any sermon or teaching on this passage must deal head-on with any conception of the Christian gospel or of a profit margin that privileges wealth in monetary terms. What is clear, however, is that Paul understands the problem of wealth in ways similar to contemporary philosophers, such as the Stoics, whose concerns with materialism or what we might call "consumerism" were located within the person. What we think about wealth and how these thoughts come to order or reorder our lives and relationships with God and our neighbors according to its acquisition is at issue.

This is why Paul repeats the wisdom that drives his economics: the profit margin that really counts—the "great profit" (6:6)—are those purchases made for eternity. The repeated catalogues of virtues (in contrast with related catalogues of vices) found in this passage underscore the importance of "saving treasury-bonds that provide a good foundation for what is truly life" (6:19). This is the life's pursuit—this cultivation of virtuous habits—of "God's man" (6:11), in this case in reference to Timothy but reapplied by sermon or class lecture to every Jesus follower.

Sermon sketch

The following three sayings from this chapter may help organize a three-point sermon on this topic.

1. *Godliness combined with contentment brings great profit* (6:6). The therapist's suggestions to guide a quest for personal contentment has become increasingly prominent in a world in which we are constantly on the alert for the ravages of climate change, pandemics, and financial uncertainty. We awake each day to news of wars, racial and sexual violence, and divisions of every kind that fracture our relationships and communities. These are days filled with crisis and change when it is very difficult to be contented with life as it is. The stress we experience intensify the burdens we feel.

The evidence is clear that working or buying our way out of the unsettled discontent we may feel—the making of more money to buy more toys or to work feverishly without concern for others to achieve a promotion to a higher rank—does not produce a grounded life without need of new direction or additional funds. Paul envisions a different perspective on contentment, which C. S. Lewis perhaps had in mind when describing Satan's principal invention as a kind of happiness whose source is apart from God—the quest for contentment routed by some path that does not also end in God. For this reason John Wesley with stunning frequency linked holiness (which has Paul's idea of *eusebius* in mind) and happiness in his preaching ministry.

2. *Compete the good race of life, lay hold of eternal life* (6:12). Paul uses a sporting typology to help Timothy capture the wisdom of his exhortation to "lay hold of eternal life." This may surprise a Protestant membership of a congregation or classroom familiar with a different formula of eternal life that requires only a profession of faith in the risen Christ's atoning work rather than also the self-sacrificial discipline of "laying hold" of God. (And here I would argue that it is the formation of God-like *character* that Paul has in view; note 6:11.)

In addition to the examples drawn from the gospel of Jesus's faithful life of righteousness and love (see the virtue list of 6:11), preachers and teachers who follow sports will easily find examples of dedicated athletes whose hard work in training has paid off in competitive victory. Care must be taken, however, to ground such illustrations of "laying hold" of eternal life lest it becomes detached from the fearless and "good confessions" the disciple also must make in following the example of Christ.

3. *Save up a treasure for the future to lay hold of what is truly life* (6:19). What a spectacular way of concluding an exhortation focused on the continuing conflict between our quest for the material treasures of "mammon" and financial security and the heavenly treasures of a vital life with God and eternal security! Akin to the book of Acts, in which the "community of shared goods" is thematic of the church being the church, Paul's definition of "what is truly life" concludes from an exhortation directed at Timothy's urban congregation's wealthy membership to "do good" by generously sharing their riches with others (6:17–18; cf. 2:10). A life of self-sacrificial generosity not only testifies to Christ's self-sacrificial love for others, it also is a discipline that forms resistance to those "senseless and harmful passions" that lead the self-centered to their ruin and destruction (6:9).

Preaching and teaching scripture's paraenetic literature provides congregations with a course in divine wisdom—a fresh way of rethinking the workplaces and public squares of the secular worlds we inhabit—that not only cultivates contentment within oneself but also a way of living that helps to reorder reality according to the divine economy (cf. 1:4–5).

2 TIMOTHY

A Snapshot of 2 Timothy

Read within its canonical context, 2 Timothy continues Paul's correspondence with his trusted delegate and successor, Timothy. The sequence of 1 and 2 Timothy commends the benedictory of 1 Timothy (6:19–20) as a hinge passage that shifts the reader's attention away from instructions that guide the formation of a congregation to instructions that form its spiritual leader—the "man of God" (2 Tim 3:17) able to preserve Paul's apostolic tradition for the next generation (cf. 2 Tim 1:13–14; 2:1–2). For this reason, 2 Timothy is more person-centered than 1 Timothy. While statements of a self-aware Paul continue to function much like his final speeches in Acts, in which he defends his importance for the church's future (e.g., Acts 20:17–35), the problem this letter addresses is no longer Paul but Paul no longer. Certainly, read in canonical context, Paul no longer needs defending; his legacy needs preserving. The crisis that occasions 2 Timothy is not the manner of Timothy's succession from Paul's apostolic leadership in Ephesus but the disintegration of the faith community's memory of Paul's spiritual legacy without which subsequent generations of Christians are left without a theological and moral compass.

Two related but discrete claims follow from these observations that help guide the pastor's preaching of 2 Timothy.

First, the repeated exhortation for Timothy to remember an exemplary Paul underwrites the importance of his apostolic tradition for the future of the faith. His life and message are integral to the church's identity as an "apostolic" (i.e., a theologically orthodox) community. Second, Paul's departure occasions an apostolic succession rooted in a memory of his life and message, which is now transmitted by the community's Spirit-inspired scripture (so 2 Tim 3:14–17; cf. 2 Pet 3:15–16).

Significantly, the manner of succession is neither institutional nor ecclesial but profoundly personal: Paul's legacy is perpetuated by particular *individuals* whose calling is to "hold to a pattern of healthy teaching you have heard from me . . . and protect the good tradition" (1:13–14) for every generation (cf. 2:2) until "that day" (1:12). The added phrase, "competent to teach still others" (2:2), is thickened by the repetition of teaching-words that recall what Paul himself taught others (1:11) and so underwrites the importance of this magisterial charism and its ministry of the word for securing a people's relationship with God.

Paul Greets Timothy

1:1 From Paul, an apostle of Christ Jesus by God's will for the purpose of the promise of life realized in Christ Jesus, [2] to Timothy, dear child: grace, mercy, and peace from God the Father and Christ Jesus our Lord.

A Profile in Courage?

[3] I give thanks to God whom I serve, as did my ancestors, with a clear conscience. I remember you in my prayers day and night. [4] I long to see you, remembering your tears, so that I may be filled with joy. [5] I take hold of your earnest faith as a reminder—the kind that first found a home in your grandmother Lois and mother Eunice and I am certain is in you. [6] For this reason, I remind you to reignite God's gift that is in you through the

laying on of my hands. [7] For God did not give us a cowardly Spirit but one of power, love, and discernment.

[8] Therefore, do not be ashamed of the Lord's testimony or of mine, his prisoner. Rather, share the suffering for the gospel by the power of God: [9] God saved and called us with a holy calling, not according to our works but according to God's own purpose and grace. God gave grace to us in Christ Jesus before time began and [10] now it has been revealed through the appearing of our savior, Christ Jesus, who abolished death and illumined life and immorality. For this gospel [11] I was appointed herald, apostle and teacher; [12] for this reason I suffer as I do. But I am not ashamed; for I know the one in whom I have placed my trust and am convinced that God is strong enough to protect my tradition until that day.

[13] Hold to a pattern of healthy teaching you have heard from me with the fidelity and loyalty that are in Christ Jesus. [14] Guard the good tradition entrusted to you by the holy Spirit who lives within you.

[15] You know this: all those in Asia, including Phygelus and Hermogenes, have turned their back on me. [16] May the Lord give mercy to Onesiphorus' household, since he often refreshed me. He was unashamed of my chain, [17] but upon arriving in Rome he diligently sought and found me. [18] May the Lord give him opportunity to find mercy from the Lord on that day. And you know how well he served us in Ephesus!

Practice Resurrection!

2:1 You then, my child, be an enabler by the grace that is in Christ Jesus. [2] And pass on the things you and many other witnesses heard from me to faithful people, competent to teach still others. [3] Share the suffering like a good soldier of Christ Jesus: [4] none who soldiers gets entangled in daily affairs, so that he might please the enlisting officer. [5] Likewise, if anyone competes and does not follow the rules, he will not be crowned. [6] The hardworking farmer must receive the first share of the crop. [7] Think about what I say; for the Lord will give to you clarity in everything.

[8] Remember Jesus Christ: raised from the dead, from the family of David. This is my gospel [9] for which I suffer bad news—bound like a common criminal; but the word of God cannot be bound. [10] Because of this I endure all this for the elect, so that they may also experience salvation in Christ Jesus with eternal glory. [11] This teaching is a core belief:

For if we shared in death, we will share also in life;

[12] if we persevere, we will also share in rule;

if we deny, he will also deny us;

[13] if we are faithless, he remains faithful for he

cannot be other than what he is.

[14] Remind them of these things and warn them before the Lord to avoid disputed teachings. There is no benefit and only destroys the auditors. [15] Present yourself before God as a proven worker who unashamedly interprets the word of truth accurately. [16] Avoid profane chatter, for it will lead many into godlessness [17] and their word will have the effect of spreading gangrene. Among them are Hymenaeus and Philetus, [18] who have missed truth's target, claiming that the resurrection has already occurred and subverting the faith of some.

[19] Even so, God's firm foundation stands, displaying this marker: "The Lord knows those belonging to him," and, "Let all those calling upon the Lord's name turn away from unrighteousness." [20] That is, in an impressive house there are not only gold and silver utensils but also some made with wood and clay; some are for special uses, some for ordinary uses. [21] Therefore, if someone thoroughly cleanses himself of these teachings, he will be set apart as "special utensils," useful to the master for every good work.

[22] Stay away from the passions of youth and instead pursue righteousness, faithfulness, love, peace with those who call upon the Lord from a pure heart. [23] Avoid foolish and thoughtless discussions, since you know they produce conflicts. [24] The Lord's servant must not quarrel but should be kind toward all, able to teach, patient, [25] schooling opponents with gentleness. Perhaps God will permit them a change of mind, then knowledge of the truth, [26] and so they

will come to their senses, escaping the devil's trap that holds them captive to do his will.

3:1 Know this: the last days will be dangerous times. [2] People will love themselves and money; they will be braggarts, arrogant, blasphemers, and disobey parents. People will be ungrateful, unholy, [3] without empathy, unresponsive, and spiteful. They will lack self-control and gentleness, without love for what is good. [4] They will be traitors and reckless, deluded lovers of pleasure rather than lovers of God. [5] They will make a public appearance of godliness but will resist its power. Have nothing to do with these people. [6] Some slither into households and take control of immature women weighed down by sins and driven by various desires. [7] They are forever learning but never able to come to knowledge of the truth. [8] In the same way that Jannes and Jambres opposed Moses, so also these people oppose the truth. They ruin the mind and counterfeit the faith. [9] But like those others, they won't get very far; their foolishness will be obvious to all.

The Three Essentials of Christian Formation

[10] You, however, have closely observed me—my teaching, way of life, purpose, faith, loyalty, love, patience, [11] physical abuse, and my suffering in places like Antioch, Iconium, and Lyastra. What abuse I put up with, and the Lord rescued me from it all! [12] In fact, anyone who desires to live a godly life with Christ Jesus will be persecuted, [13] while evil people—swindlers!—become ever worse, deceiving and being deceived.

[14] You, however, stay steady in what you have learned and found convincing, knowing from whom you learned: [15] from infancy you learned the holy writings, which enable you to be wise for salvation through faith in Christ Jesus. [16] Every scripture is God-inspired and is useful for teaching, for showing mistakes, for correcting, for training rectitude, [17] so that the person of God is mature, made mature for every good work. 4:1 In the presence of God and Christ Jesus who is coming to judge the living and the dead, by his appearing and by his kingdom, I firmly command: [2] Proclaim the word! Stand ready at all times! Refute! Rebuke! Always

encourage with patient instruction! [3] For a time will come when people will not tolerate healthy teaching. Because they are self-centered, they will accumulate teachers who say what they want to hear. [4] They will turn from hearing the truth toward conspiracy theories.

[5] You, however, remain self-controlled whenever suffering bad news. Do the work of a preacher of the good news. Carry out your service fully. [6] As for me, I've already had my fill and the time of my death is at hand. [7] I have fought the fight, finished the race, kept the faith. [8] At long last there remains for me the champion's wreath for righteousness that the Lord will give me on that day. He is the just judge, not only of me but of all those who have loved his appearance.

Final Instructions and Greetings

[9] Do you best to come to me quickly; [10] Demas, who is in love with the present world, has deserted me and has gone to Thessalonika. Crescens has gone to Galatia, Titus to Dalmatia. [11] Only Luke is with me. After you pick up Mark, bring him with you; he has been very useful in serving me. [12] I sent Tychichos to Ephesus. [13] When you come, bring the coat I left with Carpus in Troas, also the books and especially the parchments. [14] Alexander the Coppersmith has done me great harm: the Lord will repay his deeds. [15] Watch out for him, for he opposes our teaching. [16] No one took my side at my first defense; everyone deserted me. May it not be charged against them! [17] The Lord took my side and enabled me so that the message might be brought to fulfillment through me that all nations might hear it. I was also rescued from the lion's mouth; [18] the Lord will rescue me from every evil act and save me for his heavenly kingdom. To him be the glory forever and ever, amen. [19] Greet Prisca, Aquila, and the household of Onesiphorus. [20] Erastus stayed in Corinth, and I left a sick Trophimus in Miletus. [21] Do your best to come before winter. Eubulus, Pudens, Linus, Claudia, and all the brothers send greetings.

And a Concluding Prayer

[22] The Lord be with your spirit. Grace be with you all.

Chapter 6

A PROFILE IN COURAGE?

Exegetical Notes on 2 Timothy 1

1. TYPICAL OF HIS letters, Paul's personal greetings are followed by a note of thanksgiving to God that often includes a prayer for his letter's recipients. What he remembers in his prayers signals why he is writing the letter and so his petition orders the instruction that follows. Significantly, the phrase *charin echō* ("I give thanks," 1:3) is found only here and in 1 Tim 1:12, where Paul thanks Christ for his conversion and calling as a minister of the gospel. The resulting intertext of personal thanksgiving forges a way of reading 1–2 Timothy together: the sender (Paul), grateful for his apostleship (1 Timothy), expresses gratitude for a well-prepared successor to continue his apostolic faith for the spiritual formation of others as death approaches (2 Timothy).

2. Thanksgiving always occasions a remembrance of the past. Gratitude to God is expressed for gifts already received. Paul's repeated invocation of his memories in this letter seems more urgent because his death is imminent (cf. 4:6). This letter's many personal reminiscences is a literary convention of testamentary genre, which has led many interpreters to read 2 Timothy as Paul's "last will and testament" written for his spiritual heir. While perhaps so, scripture is full of personal remembrances that rather intend to present role models to imitate. In this case, Paul is less concerned about his death than he is in Timothy's preparation for pastoral ministry that follows his example. This manner of imitation recognizes that Timothy is not called to be another Paul, whose calling and charisma

are uniquely his alone (cf. Titus 1:3; 1 Tim 1:10–11); rather, for Timothy to follow Paul's example is for him to cultivate the same personal virtues and hone the same practices of ministry.

3. The verbal idea, translated "reignite" (*anazōpokriteō*), interplays with the verb used to cue the memory of shared experiences (*anamimnēskō*), the one *ana-* interacting with the other: the potential ignition of "God's gift that is in (Timothy)" is underwritten by Paul's reminiscence of his "earnest faith." The exegetical task is to define more carefully the nature of Timothy's gift and why Paul should say it needs reignition. Some commentators find here a mirror image of Timothy's self-doubt. Paul's exhortation of a "reignited" gift refers to a Timothy who lacks the confidence to get on with the demands of pastoral ministry. I am suspicious of any mirror reading that internal evidence does not support—as is the case here; the mention of Timothy's spiritual gift, however, recalls other discussions of *charismata* in Paul's other letters (Rom 12; 1 Cor 12–14) that may help readers understand this text. God's Spirit allocates gifts to individuals to empower their loving ministry within the body of Christ, with an aim of bringing every believer to spiritual maturity (cf. 1 Cor 12:4–11). The spiritual maturity and unity of Christian fellowship depends upon the community's capacity to discern the work of the Spirit in its midst and to distinguish it from the range of religious practices that flood the marketplace. Clearly from this correspondence the agent of *charisma* is the holy Spirit who not only enables the church to confess that "Jesus is Lord" (1 Cor 12:3; cf. Rom 10:9) but also allocates a variety of *charismata* according to God's will in fashioning what benefits the whole church—crucial for a ministry of reconciliation within a community conflicted over rival claims (cf. 1 Cor 1:10–12). Read with these Pauline texts, the Pauline exhortation to "reignite" a divine charisma confirms Timothy's call to bring other believers to spiritual maturity. Moreover, Timothy's charisma comes with the Spirit whose "power" (rather than Timothy's inborn or acquired talents) animates his gift and makes it effective for the public ministry to which he is called (cf. 1 Tim 1:3; 3:15–16; 4:14–16; 6:20–21).

4. The final word that characterizes the indwelling Spirit's performance is "discernment" (*sōphonismos*). Its root meaning describes the effect of an intellectual competency that enables someone to weigh competing goods and decide rightly between them. If love and power are readily understood from its Pauline co-text in 1 Corinthians, this third attribute provides a control or constraint that guarantees the powerful

and loving performance of Timothy's gifts of ministry. Paul uses this word only here but it trades on the expansive *sōphron*-word family used often in the PE. Most are found in the various virtue lists Paul uses to characterize believers capable of "good works," the hallmark of a faithful people. So, for example, the repetition of the adjective *sophrosyne* (prudence) in 2:9 and 2:15 brackets Paul's instructions to signal the essential quality of faithful women whom God will save. Read in context, then, Paul's mention of a discerning use of spiritual gifts recalls a much broader valence of the indwelling Spirit whose presence enables gifted individuals like Timothy to discern how best to use their gifts of ministry.

5. The practice of "the laying on of hands" (cf. 1 Tim 4:14) is borrowed from Judaism where it was used as a liturgical gesture during the ordination of rabbis. This gesture not only symbolized the transfer of spiritual authority to those selected to lead but was also used as confirmation that these individuals have the résumé of training and good works to lead. In this setting, the "hands" belong to Paul, who ordains his handpicked protégé and by his apostolic authority confirms the Spirit's gift. Simply put, this is a gesture of apostolic succession rather than simply an imposition of hands such as found in Acts 8:17 when Peter and John "handed off" the Spirit to repentant Samaritans. Nonetheless, this connection with Acts 8:17 may supply an added layer of meaning to this text. In Acts 8:17, as well as in 9:17–18 and 19:6, the gesture of the laying on of hands signals the baptism of the Spirit, not only as a confirmation of salvation from sin (8:17–18; 19:6; cf. 2:38) but also to empower Christian ministry (9:17–18). The laying on of Paul's hands, then, assumes that Timothy's succession comes with the Spirit's power and gift for ministry to imitate Paul in his absence; it is a succession of the Spirit of apostleship.

6. The repetition of "tradition" (*parathēkē*, 1:12, 14), which continues Paul's exhortation that concludes 1 Timothy (cf. 1 Tim 6:20) and binds these two letters together, clarifies the essential goods of Timothy's succession of Paul as well as the ultimate importance of continuing his "pattern of healthy teaching" (1:13) for the future of the church (cf. Acts 20:29–35). Paul's appointment as "herald, apostle and teacher" (1:11; cf. 1 Tim 2:7) carries with it a sacred trust that has been protected by God (1:12b) and now is passed on to Timothy for safekeeping with the Spirit's help (1:14). Rather than reading 2 Timothy as Paul's "last will and testament" as many do (see above), this should be read with 1 Timothy as a *correspondence of succession* that sets out a pattern of instruction received

from Paul (1:13) that will be used by all future leaders to catechize the church into the apostolic faith (cf. 2:2).

7. Timothy's shame-free confidence in the apostolic tradition and in the importance of his ministry to pass it on to others is predicated on what God has already achieved at "the appearing of our Savior, Christ Jesus" (1:10), which is now protected by the Spirit (1:14). This proto-Trinitarian formulation of an active God, a saving Christ, and an empowering Spirit supplies the theological soil in which the movement of the apostolic tradition is rooted. The claim that Christ Jesus is "our Savior" who "appeared" to defeat death is exceptional apart from the PE. Many saviors have been put forward, ancient and contemporary, political and religious. Paul uses "Savior" of Jesus in Phil 3:20 with evident political meaning. Paul's Roman and Jewish worlds loved and told tales of the grand appearances of legendary heroes. Even today, we populate our symbolic worlds with valorized political leaders and even present them as "saviors," whether from economic disaster, terrorist threat, or fake news. Their public "appearances" occasion considerable pomp and circumstance. Implicit in the politics of Paul is that true believers must *never* negotiate dual "citizenship" (*to politeuma*) that splits loyalties between the powers of the present age and the triune God who providentially guides the world toward the coming age of life and immortality (cf. Phil 3:18–20).

8. The summary of the gospel Paul heralds is spread across a long and complex sentence that consists mostly of participial phrases in aorist tense to secure its truth as definitive (see 1:9–10). The gospel is the means by which this truth comes "to light" (*phōtizō*). The repetition of "gospel" brings two ideas together. If suffering (and shame) results from a ministry of the gospel, then suffering is justified by the gospel's critical role: its proclamation discloses the truth about God's salvation without which people would die without "life and immortality."

The experience of suffering and the prospect of shame signal an important subtext of this letter: the preaching of the gospel provokes a political disturbance. This is so not because Paul's mission is directly opposed to Roman rule; the book of Acts makes this clear. Rather it is because the embrace of the gospel forges a radical vision of life and daily practices that threaten the empire's way of doing business. The juxtaposition of the "power of God" and the believer's "suffering for the gospel" is a political declaration (1:8), which implies that a life molded by a Pauline "pattern of healthy teaching" under the aegis of the indwelling Spirit constitutes a real problem for those holders of secular power. Of course, Paul makes clear that his gospel does not summon the congregation to political revolution; it rather announces the epiphany of a savior, who is Jesus (1:10) and not one of Rome's pretenders to his messianic throne.

9. The idiom of time in this exhortation is important to note. A succession of leadership brings the past of the departing leader into tension with the present successor's movement into an unknown future, focused on whether there will be a continuity of the sacred. Paul speaks not only of his past proclamation of the gospel about what "now been revealed" in the coming of Christ Jesus (1:10) but also of God's economy of grace that began "before time" (1:9; cf. Rom 8:28–30; 1 Cor 2:7; Eph 1:4) to make good on a "promise of life" for those who are "in Christ Jesus" (cf. 1:1).

This memory of his apostleship forges a sacred tradition passed on to Timothy until Jesus returns (1:12). The apocalyptic catchphrase, "until that day," which Paul uses often and often strategically (see 1:18; 4:8; cf. Rom 2:16; 13:12; 1 Cor 1:8; 1 Thess 5:4; 2 Thess 1:10), refers to a future, finite, and final date of reckoning when Judge God will demand a rigorous accounting of everyone's faithfulness. The repetition of this phrase in the following positive example of Onesiphorus' household (cf. 1:18) suggests that its sense here is to underwrite Timothy's faithful succession for which he will be rewarded by God on "that day."

10. The phrase "pattern of healthy teaching" concludes Paul's exhortation about Timothy's succession. Although exceptional in the NT, the word "pattern" (*hypotyposis*) had broad currency in the Greco-Roman world when referring to a summary or outline of someone's teaching. Not only is an exemplary Paul worthy of imitation, "pattern" carries a curricular pressure much like the first collection of Pauline letters that was probably put into circulation as the theological curriculum of new believers.[1] Paul's use of *hypotypōsis* within an exhortation about "healthy teachings" suggests that Timothy's training may have been ordered by a collection of Paul's letters that could have been recycled to teach the teachers of the tradition to preserve it for the next generation of the church (cf. 2:2).

While Timothy's reception of what he has received from and observed of Paul's own commitment to his sacred calling as "herald (*kērux*; cf. 1 Tim 2:7), apostle, and teacher" of the gospel (1:11) forge his understanding of his own gift and so also the practices of his charism in forming a congregation, the pair of imperatives to "hold" and "protect" this "healthy teaching"

---

1. Trobisch, *Paul's Letter Collection.*

presumes that Timothy's theological education will take roots only if the messenger is worthy of this apostolic message. Timothy's earnest faith in God (cf. 1:5) and his loving relations for others (cf. 1 Tim 1:5) secures Paul's confidence that he will pass on his teaching to others (2:2).

Preaching 2 Timothy 1

Sermon big idea

The chapter title, "A Profile in Courage," trades on the famous collection of short biographies of influential US senators written by President John F. Kennedy in the 1950s. It is a purposefully ironical portal into 2 Timothy 1 focused by the somewhat tentative way Paul seeks to encourage his beloved and gifted but reluctant protegee, Timothy. This is among scripture's most important passages on a believer's "holy calling" (1:9), a topic much discussed but rarely in conversation with scripture's more didactic texts. Stories of biblical figures who are called to serve God are used as substitutes for biblical texts like this one that offer canonical instructions to guide and direct those ordained to Christian ministry (cf. 1:6b). This passage regards the sacred call of those gifted for ministry, which perhaps can be applied to an entire congregation called by God to testify by word and life to the truth of gospel, sometimes at great cost (1:8b).

Sermon sketch

There are three interpenetrating texts in this chapter that work together to present a sermon or lecture on God's sacred call to ministry.

1. *"I remind you to reignite God's gift that is in you"* (1:6a). Any sermon on this chapter should focus on Paul's remarkable exhortation to Timothy to "reignite" God's gift given to him, which in his case was confirmed by apostolic ordination. While no indication is given of Timothy's neglect of the tasks he is charged to do as Paul's delegate, there is a hard realism in Paul's carefully chosen reminder to engage in the gospel ministry assigned him with confidence and without shame. Many pundits have noted that an increasingly secular culture has become less passive and more outspoken about its opposition to theism of every kind. Christians in particular have been "shamed" and blamed for creating a hostile environment for any who chose a lifestyle at odds with a consensus of Christian teaching

on a wide range of ethical and intellectual topics. The repetition of shame and suffering language in this passage in connection with Paul's practice of the Christian gospel suggests a similar opposition, confirmed by a prior reading of Paul's story in Acts. Rather than engage in culture-bashing, perhaps a more basic recognition of the radical nature of Paul's gospel set out in 1:9–10, especially since it concentrates on the cruciformed Christ, is needed to understand Timothy's possible timidity and Paul's exhortation that our witness is empowered by the Spirit who also safeguards or takes responsibility for its effective communication.

2. *"For this gospel I was appointed herald, apostle, and teacher"* (1:11). This triad of gospel practices repeats Paul's affirmation of himself in 1 Tim 2:7 and probably indicates canonical markers of an apostolic appointment. A sermon/lecture on this chapter should avoid expansive word studies of what each entails and rather make the point that such practices underscore the importance of the content of communication that is heralded and taught by someone appointed an apostle (or prophet). That is, in making this second point one might begin with 1:11 but then work backward in helping a congregation or classroom understand the terms of the apostolic gospel heralded and taught according to 1:9–10. There is hardly a more sufficient summary of Paul's gospel than this one; in many ways, it offers readers of the Pauline corpus a handy abstract for finding the theological goods in any Pauline letter (in my view, especially Romans).

3. *"Guard the good tradition entrusted to you by the holy Spirit who lives within us"* (1:14). The final point of this sermon might be nicely introduced by William Faulkner's famous line in his *Requiem for a Nun* that "the past is never dead. It's not even past." This is a sermon concentrated by the importance of a ministry in continuity with the past—with the church's inheritance of a past filled and funded by sacred texts and memories of gifted saints. The effective performance of God's gifted ministers of the gospel depends largely on whether their ministry continues to herald and teach others what they have been taught from the church founded on its apostolic witness. It should not go unnoticed that the practice of Paul's apostleship is sandwiched between his work as "herald" and "teacher" of Christ Jesus in 2 Timothy's succinct description of his divine appointment. The "tradition" that has provided Timothy (and so also today's ministers of the gospel) with words that form a healthy, spiritually vital community of faith—one that continues to be supported and safeguarded by the holy Spirit—is founded on a pattern of instruction learned from the apostle. Implicit in the church's

affirmation that it is "one holy catholic and *apostolic*" is that its existence and ongoing testimony presumes a ministry that safeguards its apostolic past received in the apostolic writings canonized in its scripture.

Chapter 7

PRACTICE RESURRECTION!

Exegetical Notes on 2 Timothy 2

1. THIS CHAPTER OPENS by reprising the central theme of 1–2 Timothy: Timothy's succession of Paul. In this instance, Paul tells Timothy to instruct his successors in what he had heard from him (2:1–2). The opening "you then" is emphatic and relates the following triad of imperatives—be strong, pass on, share the suffering—applies the preceding example of Onesophorus to Timothy: even as Onesophorus served an imprisoned Paul (cf. 1:15–18) so also should Timothy serve Paul by passing on what the apostle had taught him to others. The repetition of the letter's opening address, "my child" (see 1:2; cf. 1 Tim 1:18) reminds Timothy that his role in this apostolic succession is family business.

I translate the first imperative "be an enabler" (*endynamoō*) to recall Paul's earlier reminder that the Spirit indwelled Timothy both as gift-giver to enable his ministry (cf. 1:6–7) and to aid him in protecting and passing on the apostolic tradition received from Paul (cf. 1:14). I translate the prepositional phrase instrumentally ("by the grace") rather than as a source of Timothy's power that enables him to perform those tasks delegated to him in the apostle's absence.

The second imperative puts this matter plainly: Timothy is to "pass on" to others what he and other "witnesses" have heard the apostle say. For the church fathers, this exhortation, along with 1 Tim 6:20 and 2 Tim 1:13–14, form the biblical imperative for an ecclesial episcopacy whose responsibility it was to maintain and manage an unbroken and indissoluble connection with the Lord's apostles and their witness of the incarnate "Word of life" (cf. 1 John 1:1–3). This doctrine of apostolic succession provided a principal theological warrant for the church's "rule of faith" and its use as the *norma normans*—a "rule that rules"—by which the episcopacy could measure publicly and consistently any claim for theological orthodoxy.

I translate the third imperative, although a single verb, "share the suffering," repeating Paul's earlier charge to "share the suffering for the gospel" in imitation of both him and "our Lord" (1:8). This imperative is elaborated by a threefold illustration (2:3–7) that makes clear the personal expense of Timothy's task. It is the gospel's claims that are provocative, not Paul or Timothy's persona (cf. 1:6–8). If his apostolic legacy, however, includes memories of Paul's mission, then suffering is the expected expense paid by those who follow him. The question remains, however, what manner of suffering does Paul envisage, whether martyrdom, shame, or still some other species?

2. The aorist form of the verb, *akouō* ("heard") opens Paul's critical statement about succession. The idea of passing on what was learned by listening attentively to him recalls 1:13 where what is heard from Paul is a "pattern of healthy teaching." This is the content, then, of what Timothy "passes on" to "many other witnesses," who in this way "hear" Paul afresh.

The phrase could be understood instrumentally so that Timothy's religious formation as Paul's witness is succeeded by "many witnesses." Two adjectives are used to identify these witnesses and their continuity with the apostle: they are faithful and competent. Not surprisingly, the quality of "faithful" instruction is measured by Paul's example in the PE (cf. 1 Tim 1:12, 15; 4:10, 12; 5:16). A second adjective, "competent," is a more practical quality and concerns the effectiveness in learning what is taught but then also in teaching others, which is thematic of the PE.

3. Timothy surely understands in general terms the task at hand: he is a custodian of memories that map a Pauline pattern of instruction, which he has been delegated to pass on to these competent others in Paul's absence. The imperative "share the suffering" cues the personal and political expense of this body of work, which even though conducted in the company of the indwelling Spirit is culpable to acts of unfaithfulness and the treachery of others. What may surprise the reader is that Timothy's imitation of Paul's suffering does not seem to suggest the same kind of experience, e.g., that Timothy will follow Paul into prison (cf. 1:8) or suffer the same physical

abuse Paul suffered during his mission to the nations (cf. 3:11). The profiles in courage included here are of competent professionals whose personal sacrifice and hard work pay dividends of excellence—a kind of "no pain, no gain" approach required for a successful succession.

The first profile is of the disciplined soldier (2:3–4). The evident intention is not to endorse professional soldiering as a Christian profession! The "good soldier" rather illustrates the kind of faithfulness (and competence) Paul has in mind: exact attentiveness to the chain-of-command (Christ-Paul-Timothy-others) is a well-known illustration in the Roman world of suffering that follows from a soldier's faithfulness to the chain of command and performance that pleases the one who "recruits" (or "calls"; cf. 1:6–7) him.

The second profile is of the athlete (2:5) whose game-plan is similar to that of the soldier. In antiquity, as today, the athlete's faithful attention to the rules of the game or to a regimen of training is necessary for victory (cf. 2:10–13; 4:8). In this case, faithfulness and competence are linked to following the rules. The subtext of *nomimōs*, which I translate "follow the rules," probably includes the rigorous preparation required of a good athlete. Paul uses this same word in 1 Tim 1:8 when speaking of a "lawful" use of the rule of law to criticize Torah teachers who make claims without the preparation needed to teach the word of truth rightly (see 2:15).

The third profile of the hardworking farmer (2:6) is also used in antiquity of someone worthy of imitation (cf. 1 Cor 9:7, 10; Jas 5:7). The word order of this text privileges the farmer's toil (*kopiōnta*) over his reward, even though the two are integrally linked: good work begets a bumper crop. Again, the exhortation to "share the suffering" is linked to hard work. Timothy's suffering results from doing the work Paul instructs, which is a condition of future victory (see 4:8; cf. 1 Tim 4:13–16).

The phrase that concludes this triad of examples is puzzling (2:7). Perhaps it best to understand it either as a tagline similar to the "Amen" that notes a hymn's end or a portal through which Timothy, made wiser by this triad, enters into his future ministry.

4. The next pericope (2:8–13) begins with a reminder of a core belief of Paul's gospel: "Jesus Christ [is] raised from the dead" (2:8). Chrysostom rightly wonders why Paul would encourage Timothy to "remember Jesus Christ" (2:8a), but concludes that it must be "directed chiefly against the heretics, at the same time to encourage Timothy by underscoring the divine blessings accompanying sufferings, since Christ, our Master, himself

overcame death by suffering" (*Homilies on 2 Timothy* 4). In this letter, the exhortation "to remember" introduces the gospel's core beliefs, which surely must include Jesus' "resurrection from the dead" and his messianic credential as a "descendent of David" (cf. Rom 1:3–4).

The form of Paul's exhortation, however, strikes me as odd: the name "Jesus Christ" is unprecedented in this letter and may suggest that it is borrowed from an early Christian creed known to Timothy. Read in context of the Pauline corpus, the reader expects the historical sequence of Rom 1:3–4 where mention is made of Jesus' Davidic descent followed by his resurrection (and exaltation) as God's Son. But this new sequence prioritizes the Lord's bodily resurrection, perhaps anticipating the problem of Hymenaeus and Philetus (see 2:18) and to underscore suffering as a resurrection practice. The mention of Jesus's Davidic lineage, which seems unnecessary in this setting, may allude to Jesus's kingship (so Matthew's Gospel), a notion especially provocative to imperial Rome, which helps explain Paul's suffering "like a common criminal" (2:10).

5. The interplay of three powerful contrasts convey the extent of Paul's suffering for Christ's sake. First, is the contrast between Paul's proclamation of "good news" (*euangelion*) and his personal experience of "bad news" (*kakopatheō*; lit. "bad suffering"). Second, this experience of "bad (*kakos*) news" is elaborated by citizen Paul's treatment as a "common criminal" (*kakourgos*, lit. "bad-doer"). These two contrasts frame a third: the dramatic irony between a "bound" Paul and the unbound word of God. Paul recognizes that he (and by implication, Timothy) is but a human agent who serves a divine purpose (cf. 1 Tim 2:3–7). The relationship between Paul's suffering and his gospel ministry is made clear in 2:10. In fact, those ushered into God's salvation during his evangelistic crusades are the fruit of his suffering! That is, the power of God's salvation mediated by his gospel is not *in spite of* his suffering and imprisonment but *because of* it.

6. The passing mention of "the elect" retrieves an important OT trope of Israel as God's chosen people (cf. Exod 19:3–6). The modern discussion of a Protestant conception of election is hopelessly muddled in the offense of its particularity: if only certain people are the "elect" of God and saved from sin, then most people are not and have no chance of eternal life. But scripture's theology of election, especially witnessed in the ancestral narratives of Genesis, is not interested in this theodicy but with how people respond to God's plan to save the world (cf. 1 Tim 3–7). The theological point of election does not concern the identity of those to whom salvation

belongs but the surety of God's unrelenting promise to show mercy to God's covenant people who now reside "in Christ Jesus," who by faith will in fact "experience salvation with eternal glory" (2:10).

7. Christian existence is formed by participation with the risen Christ (2:11–13). The saying added in 2:11–13 is as complex as it is gapped. It consists of four conditional statements expressed by verbs without subjects or objects. To fill in these gaps and add the substantive markers to this saying, the reader must "remember Jesus Christ" who "is raised from the dead, from the family of David" (2:8a). In fact, the very purpose of the elative "for" that introduces this saying is to unpack the implication of this confession for Christian existence.

The programmatic conditional, introduced as a "core belief" (2:11a)—sayings spread across the PE that summarize a Pauline theology of salvation—asserts that "for if we shared in death, we share also in life" (2:11b), presumes a Pauline interpretation of the dying and rising of Christ and the believer's participation with him in their experience of newness of life (Rom 6:1–14; 1 Thess 4:17). The second and third conditionals form a parallelism based upon verbal tenses to expand upon Paul's participatory Christology. According to this parallelism, the present experience of Christian fidelity (protasis) yields a realistic hope for future blessing (apodosis). If each line presumes the opening affirmation of the risen Christ, the second line would read, "if we persevere (present indicative) with Christ, we will also participate in his rule (future indicative)." Further, the repetition of *syn-* ("with") verbs spread across these first two conditionals fashions a normative chronology of Paul's participatory Christology: to die with (past), to live with (present), and to rule with Christ (future), which some think was a formula Paul used in Christian baptism.[1]

8. The third (and controversial) conditional, "if we deny (Christ), he will also deny us" (2:12b), retains this same dynamic between present and future but in negative terms as a warning against disaffection—again in anticipation of his sharp rebuke of Hymenaeus and Philetus as "gangrene" (2:16–18). Their message puts them outside the "elect" and imperils their "eternal glory" (2:10, 19). If, however, Paul's topic continues to be his apostolic succession, the dangerous consequence of denying Pauline teaching about the risen Jesus Christ motivates a warning to Timothy to teach "the word of truth" about the risen Jesus accurately and not fall prey to false teaching (cf. 2:15). The idea that Timothy's salvation is conditioned upon

---

1. Collins, *1 & 2 Timothy and Titus*, 226–27.

his performance of ministerial practices is already found in 1 Tim 4:14–16 and may be implicit here. The Lord's faithfulness to a promise made is undeniable on evidence of the resurrection; and so the warning implicit in this line should be read in a qualified way: God's preferential option is always for the remediation and repentance of the faithless. The prospect of God's denial of a believer's "eternal glory" must be seen as a last resort when every effort of correction, whether mediated by the apostle or the Satan (see 1 Tim 1:19–20), is refused.

9. Paul departs from this negative pattern in the apodosis of the fourth conditional (2:13) to conclude on a positive note: Christ's resurrection evinces his faithfulness to God and to God's promise of eternal life made to the elect community. Sharply put, whether or not a gifted and ordained Timothy chooses to continue Paul's gospel ministry does not influence God's election of a faithful people for eternal life. Implicit in Paul's affirmation of Christ's faithfulness is that what Timothy (or other potential successors of Paul's ministry) is capable of doing—i.e., denying the gospel's truth—the exalted Christ is unable to do: he remains faithful to God (see Hebrews).

10. The injunction, "remind them" (2:14), introduces a triad of practices undertaken by the congregation's leader: "remind . . . warn . . . avoid" (2:14). In particular, the congregation is warned to avoid false teachers whose pedagogy and instruction do not follow the pattern of Pauline instruction (cf. 2 Tim 1:13–14) and so are subversive of the community's participation with Christ in salvation (2:15–18). Positively, Timothy is advised to be a hard "worker" with a "proven" résumé (*dokemos*, 2:15a) that can pass God's review in which faithfulness, competence, and self-sacrifice (cf. 2:2–3a) are needed when teaching others to teach others the "word of truth" (2:15b). On this basis one might anticipate a positive result. But the plain emphasis here is on the character of workers, forged during a costly discipleship, and on the content of their instruction, both of which must pass God's test for excellence.

11. Images of the daily laborer are found throughout the NT (e.g., Gospel parables, 1 Tim 5:18; Jas 5:4; Acts 19:25) to illustrate the virtues of hard work. In this case, Timothy's hard work is to "interpret" (*orthotomeō*, lit. to "make a right path," cf. Prov 3:6; 11:5) the "word of truth" without apology (2:15) since a word on target safeguards the tradition and leads one to salvation (cf. 2 Tim 3:15). Characteristically Paul notes that the content and pedagogy of a message of truth contrasts with that of false

teachers. He rarely names his opponents or describes what they teach in the PE; he rather uses them as rhetorical foils to clarify what should be taught and the manner of doing so (e.g., 1 Tim 4:1–4). Yet in this instance Hymenaeus (cf. 1 Tim 1:20) and Philetus are named as Timothy's counterexamples: they have departed from a Pauline proclamation of resurrection (cf. 1 Cor 15:12).

The implicit contrast between a "healthy (or Pauline) teaching" (so 1 Tim 1:10; 6:3; cf. 1:13) and the spread of gangrene creates a vivid wordplay of the putrefaction that results in a congregation's spiritual formation when its teachers depart from Pauline orthodoxy: heresy putrefies spiritual health. And the mention of this pair of troublemakers, whose reputation is no doubt familiar to the reader, may well be a rhetorical ploy to indicate their potential for wreaking havoc, which only intensifies the urgency of Paul's exhortation to Timothy to remind and warn members to avoid their influence (2:14) and instead listen keenly to the word of truth (2:15).

Although a few manuscripts of 2 Timothy use an indefinite "a resurrection" (cf. 2:18) of some unspecified resurrection being taught, I prefer the articular form, "the resurrection," since the very mention of Hymenaeus and Philetus presumes that Timothy would have known their misinterpretation of Paul's teaching and its theological implication for Christian existence. This text does not discuss their teaching. Most interpreters trade on the prior saying in concluding that they have promised an escape from present suffering (cf. 2:10)—a ancient version of today's "prosperity gospel."[2] While Paul nowhere denies today's benefits of a believer's participating with the risen Christ, his immediate concern is how our present self-sacrifice for the sake of others may be considered a resurrection practice.

12. Unlike Hymenaeus and Philetus, Timothy is a "special (*timē*) utensil" whose personal and pastoral practices (2:19–25) make is possible for the spiritual restoration of those false teachers (2:26). The emphatic "even so" (2:19) draws a necessary conclusion from 2:13: God's faithfulness to the truth of Paul's gospel remains secure. In the face of the threat posed by the rival gospel of Hymenaeus and others, then, the rock-solid referent of "God's firm foundation" remains the apostolic tradition (cf. 1 Tim 6:19–20; 1 Cor 3:10–12; Eph 2:20; also Rom 15:20) on which the congregation's faith is made secure (see 1 Tim 3:15). The first citation from LXX Num 16:5 recalls the story of Korah's (a former-day Hymenaeus) rebellion against the sacred leadership of Moses (a former-day Paul) and Aaron (a former-day

---

2. Marshall, *The Pastoral Epistles*, 771–74.

Timothy) that adds an important layer of meaning to the reader's understanding of what is at stake in this current conflict. Korah and his Levitical colleagues demanded shared authority with the Aaronic priesthood. But Israel is not a democracy; it is ruled over by God alone and Korah's rebellion is finally not against Moses and Aaron but against God. The application is clear: God has appointed Paul as apostle and has entrusted him with God's glorious gospel (see 1 Tim 1:11) as the means of salvation. Hymenaeus and Philetus are neither apostles nor Paul's successors; they have no portfolio from God to define the word of truth that saves.

13. The analogy of the "impressive house" (2:20–21) recalls Paul's expansive use of the "household" metaphor in the PE to alert their readers that this "house" refers to congregations who have received the word of truth (esp. 1 Tim 3:15). Utensils made of precious materials for use on special occasions refer to members with "special" gifts (e.g., Timothy) to enable "special uses" (e.g., to safeguard Paul's apostolic tradition). One also expects to find in any household those utensils made of "wood and clay" (i.e., ordinary materials) for everyday use. Likewise, one would expect to find rank-and-file members whose gifts suit a congregation's more mundane work. I have translated the Greek phrase, *eis atimian*, "for ordinary use," to refer to utensils made with wood and clay. The common (and plausible) translation of this phrase is cast in moral terms—"for dishonor" (KJV, NASB) or "for ignoble use" (NIV, NET)—which tries to press the analogy to make a moral contrast between Paul and his opponents or even between God and the devil (cf. 2:25b–26). There is no indication here, however, that Paul divides the membership in this way. Here Paul wants Timothy to embrace his "honorable use" (so 1:6–8) as a carrier of the "word of truth."

14. The final pericope of this chapter (2:22–26) continues this theme. Paul catalogues the honorable practices and virtues of a "special utensil" in God's service. The initial exhortation to "pursue righteousness," with its complement of virtues, repeats these same attributes of Christian existence found elsewhere in the PE. "Peace" is found only in the opening salutation (cf. 1 Tim 1:2; 2 Tim 1:2) and so its use here may highlight a particular kind of peace-keeping that avoids those "foolish and thoughtless discussions" that produce interpersonal "heat" rather than knowledge of the truth (2:23–25). The word translated "thoughtless" is the antonym of *paideuō*, a kind of "schooling" that brings even Paul's opponents to repentance and to a knowledge of the truth (see 1 Tim 2:4).

The prospect of an opponent's repentance signals the optimism of Paul's confidence in God's truth-telling to change minds, which is thematic of these letters (2:25; see 1 Tim 1:19–20; 2:4; 3:6–7; cf. Titus 1:1). The distinctive use of "coming to knowledge of the truth" in these two Timothy letters (1 Tim 2:4; 2 Tim 2:25; 3:7; cf. Titus 1:1) gives expression to an element central to Paul's gospel and compels a mission that combats misinformation and ignorance. A "word of truth" kindly but rationally presented is an escape route to the devil's captive to "come to their senses" (2:26).

Preaching 2 Timothy 2

Sermon big idea

Wendell Berry concludes his remarkable and evocative poem "Manifesto: The Mad Farmer Liberation Front" with the exhortation, "Practice Resurrection." His exhortation suggests that a right reading of his poem offers a fresh way—a "manifesto"—of owning belief in resurrection that carries its radical content—"something that won't compute," as he puts it—but also the promise of real-life, transformative consequences. Paul's illustrative use of various kinds of hard workers to illustrate the outworking of "the grace that is in Christ Jesus" (2:1) includes the farmer (2:6) and suits well Berry's idea of resurrection. It is a practice! While not everyone will agree with his politics or appreciate the sharp ironical turns of his platitudes, the emphasis his poem places on the real difference our choices make resonates with the focus of this chapter. The soundbites I have gathered from this chapter to score a three-point sermon underscore the *practical* importance of teaching and embodying the gospel's belief that "Jesus Christ is raised from the dead" (2:8). Preach "Practice Resurrection"!

Sermon sketch

The three points and altar call of this sermon are all focused by Paul's reminder of the central claim of his gospel set out in 2:8: "Jesus Christ, raised from the dead." This claim not only supplies the content of the message preached but also the character of the one who preaches it. These two, message and messenger, form an integral whole and define what is meant by the church's manifesto: "Practice Resurrection!"

1. *"Be an enabler by the grace that is in Christ Jesus"* (2:1). The imperatives that add urgency to its opening sentence as well as the triad of exemplars that follow alert the congregation that they are called to practice what is preached. The practice in this case is to teach others to teach others to create a chain of competence that will secure the movement of the gospel into the next generation of believers. This is hard work; it requires the discipline of a soldier, the training of an athlete, and the careful planning of a farmer.

2. *"Remember Jesus Christ, raised from the dead; this is my gospel"* (2:8). If the primary clergy practice is to partner with the holy Spirit to safeguard the apostolic tradition by teaching others to teach others, then the teacher/preacher of the tradition needs to learn it. To practice resurrection is to preach resurrection. Paul begins a series of remembrances with the charge to remember a Jesus who was raised from the dead and then provides a commentary on why this is central to his gospel—if a risen Jesus, then we "obtain salvation" (2:10): that is, we live with him, we will reign with him, and he remains faithful to the faithful (2:11–13).

3. *"Present yourself before God as a proven worker who unashamedly interprets the word of truth accurately"* (2:15). A final point in preaching this chapter offers a profile of someone with a résumé of practice that passes divine muster. The message they communicate is noted for its accuracy and directness (2:15b–16) but also by its messenger who embodies "every good work" (2:21–25a) as markers of what genuine repentance looks like at ground level (2:25b–26). It is critical that resurrection is not only preached but practiced by a faithful congregation and/or minister of the gospel.

4. *An altar call.* It should be noted that Paul offers Timothy a counter-profile in 3:1–9 of those whose self-centered practices—those who love pleasure rather than God (3:4)—fail to produce fruit in keeping with repentance. Paul's assessment is based on hard evidence: while able to "take control of the immature" (3:6), those who practice falsehoods rather than the truth produce "warped minds" and lives "weighed down by sins" (3:6) evident to everyone (3:9). What is clear throughout the PE is that the distinction between a "message" and its "messenger," often made when the flaws of the messenger are evident to all, is nowhere supported by Paul. Following the prophets, the two are of a piece: the character of the messenger must embody the claims of the message. The two are of a single, interactive piece.

Chapter 8

THE THREE ESSENTIALS OF CHRISTIAN FORMATION

Exegetical Notes on 2 Timothy 3–4

1. THE PRESENT PASSAGE is probably the most frequently interpreted and instructed exhortation of the PE. Its beginning (3:10–13), middle (3:14—4:4), and ending (4:5–8) begin with the formula *su de* ("you, however"), which not only makes Paul's address of his young apprentice emphatic but implies that Timothy's imitation of Paul's apostolic ministry would contrast with those various opponents mentioned or alluded to in the PE (cf. Acts 20:18b–21).

2. Not surprisingly the first item of the ideal résumé Paul mentions is *didaskalia* ("teaching"). The adumbration of "teaching" in the PE integrates a range of interests, including the orthodoxy of what is taught (cf. 2 Tim 1:13; 1 Tim 1:10; 4:6; 6:3), its religious purpose (cf. 1 Tim 1:5; 4:16; 2 Tim 4:3), and social manner (cf. 2 Tim 3:16; 4:13). To "closely observe" Paul's instruction is to "pass on the things you have heard from me to faithful people, competent to teach still others" (2:2). Paul's profile contrasts sharply with his opponents who follow the lead of Jannes and Jambres (cf. 3:6–9).

3. Two additional terms form the programmatic triad of essential elements to imitate: Paul's "way of life" and his driving "purpose." Although "way of life" (*agōgē*) is used only here in the NT, it is found in Paul's LXX (Esth 2:20; 10:3; 2 Macc 4:16; 6:8; 11:24; 3 Macc 4:10) and in contemporary philosophy (which was followed by the teachers of earliest

Christianity; see below; e.g., 1 Clem 47.6; 48.1). It implies not just a lifestyle but a way of understanding the world where life's way is traveled and shaped. Paul's "purpose" (*prothesei*) for teaching and guiding his way in the world recalls its earlier use in 2 Tim 1:9 of God's purpose that shapes how Paul understands his apostolate.

4. A second triad restates the familiar virtues of a Spirit-imbued life ("faith, patience [cf. 4:2], love"), while a final triad ("endurance, persecutions, sufferings" [4:10–11]) reprises themes mentioned earlier of his imprisonment and perhaps anticipate his farewell to Timothy in the final unit of this exhortation (see 4:6–8). By contextualizing Paul's canonical letters within his story in Acts the reader finds stories that elaborate his mention of "physical abuse and my sufferings . . . in places like Antioch, Iconium, and Lystra" (3:11; cf. Acts 13–14). In many ways, the rule of life implied by this passage is anticipated by a prior reading of his Miletus speech in Acts 20:18–35 in both purpose and content. In both texts, Paul distills his experiences into a general mark of Christian discipleship: "anyone who desires to live a godly life with Christ Jesus will be persecuted" (3:12; cf. Acts 14:22; 20:23–4, 29–30).

4. The addition of "evil people . . . become ever worse" (3:13), which comes from apocalypticism's playbook, locates this difficult succession during "the last days" (3:1) when evil will proliferate because of the insidious progress of bad theology (cf. 3:2–9); this, then, explains the addition of the "however" to the opening formula: "however, you, Timothy," are not like those "evil people." The naming of Jannes and Jambres, the nameless "enchanters" of the Exodus story (LXX Exod 8:18–19), recalls an important biblical subtext of Paul's résumé: in these last days before the kingdom comes (see 4:1), Timothy must never imitate those earlier "enchanters" who tricked the Pharaoh and prevented him from turning to God.

5. The second *su de* ("You, however"; 3:14) cues a related but different theme of *mimesis*: as an observant Jew, Paul practices Israel's scripture. Imitating Jesus, whose messianic interpretations of scripture led him into conflict with other biblical interpreters (cf. Matt 5:17–20), the "persecution and suffering" of the Paul of Acts is due to his messianic readings of scripture (cf. Acts 17:1–9). The issue is not over divergent Bible practices or a battle for the Bible's authority, since on these issues Paul's use of scripture is of a piece with his Jewish tradition; the issue is Jesus, whose messianic mission grinds the hermeneutical lens for his reading of Israel's scripture, but also occasions his suffering (cf. Acts 9:15–16).

6. Imitation of Paul's Bible practices requires more than skillful and Spirit-inspired interpretation; it requires a regulatory norm based on "knowing from whom you learned" (3:14b). Although the pronoun, "whom," was corrupted by copyists during transmission, most (although not the earliest) manuscripts of 2 Timothy use the singular, "from the certain one" (*para tinos*), referring only to Paul. This reading fits better the letter's portrait of a canonical Paul whose interpretation of scripture is considered normative. In fact, the repetition of "learning" (*manthanō*) makes clear the penultimate aim of Timothy's schooling is to "stay steady" (lit. "to remain") in the things learned from Paul. The motive to do so, of course, derives from the principle of imitation without which a succession of a Pauline "way of life" would not occur.

7. The precise meaning and intention of Paul's phrase "the holy writings" (3:15, *ta hiera grammata*) has provoked considerable debate. Most scholars now agree that the phrase refers to Paul's Bible: Israel's scripture in Greek translation, the Septuagint. But, additionally, Paul may have intended a more common and colloquial meaning of *grammata* (lit. "letters") referring to the ABCs of a curriculum. The added adjective "holy" would suggest, then, a *theological* or sacred curriculum in which scripture is the student's principal text.

8. The effect of learning scripture enables Timothy to become "wise for salvation through faith in Christ Jesus" (3:15b). If this second "you, however" is read as a well-rehearsed affirmation of scripture—as its rhetorical shape as a chiasm for easy recall would suggest—this happy result of salvation is located as its irreducible centerpiece (C = 15b). The parallel pairs that then encircle it list the elements that produce this result: Timothy's theological instruction (A = v. 14 and A' = v. 17) and scripture's role in his formation (B = v. 15a and B' = v. 16). Timothy's *experience* of salvation by faith in Christ Jesus (C) is the target of his Christian formation (A/A') and his use of scripture is the mechanism that forms capable lives for God (B/B').

The phrase "through faith in Christ Jesus" is quintessentially Pauline (see 1 Tim 1:14; cf. Gal 2:16; 3:26; Rom 3:22). If reading scripture enables a wisdom that saves, such a salvation is impossible apart from Christ Jesus, a core belief summarized by the various sayings spread across the PE (e.g., 1 Tim 1:15; 2 Tim 2:11–13). Affirmation of these core beliefs about Christ Jesus is prerequisite for a Christian reading of a scripture way of salvation and the reader's experience of victory over sin and death.

9. No reason is given why the term for scripture changes to *pasa graphē* ("every scripture") in 3:16. The meaning and motive for using this term is as ambiguous as the prior term for Paul's Bible: "holy writings (or letters)." They do not appear to be used interchangeably; yet "every scripture" would extend to every part of "the holy writings." If learning every part of "the holy writings" cultivates the know-how (or "wisdom") that saves, then its every performance is inspired by God to produce this saving wisdom.

10. The two most famous predicate and parallel adjectives that define what scripture is, according to scripture, are found here: every scripture is both "God-inspired" (*theopneustos*) and "useful" for forming the faith of its readers. The syntax of this famous affirmation is, however, problematic since it lacks a verb that would ordinarily relate the two adjectives to their common subject, "every scripture." The verbal sense of this affirmation trades on the present participle of *dynamai* (3:15, "is able") of the preceding affirmation. In contrast to traditional Protestant interpretation of this text, then, the action of God's inspiration of scripture is not timed in the past production of scripture at the moment of its composition but in its present uses ("teaching . . . training," 3:16b) in forming a capable Christian (cf. 3:17). "Every scripture *is* God-inspired and is useful for teaching, for showing mistakes, for correcting, for training rectitude, so that the people of God are mature, made mature for every good work."

11. The precise meaning of *theopneustos* is made more difficult by its infrequent use in antiquity: this is the only place in scripture where it is used. Quite possibly Paul created *theopneustos* by recalling two passages of his Bible in which "God" (*theos*) "breathed" (*pneuō*) new life into lifeless people. The first is Gen 2:7 when "God" (*ho theos*) breathed the "breath of life" (*pnoē zōēs*) into the first human, who "became alive." The second is Ezekiel's stunning vision of Israel's "dry bones" rattling around in the desert without life (Ezek 37:1–14). The prophet recognizes there is no "breath" (*pneuma*) in exiled Israel's corpse (37:8b) and so Israel's faithful God commissions *to pneuma* ("the spirit")—an articular noun that must refer to the Lord's spirit—to command "the fourfold spirit (*tessares pneumatos*) to breath into these corpses and they will live" (37:9b). Paul draws upon both antecedent texts to retrieve their use of the same theological trope, a breathing God, in order to connect scripture with God's impartation of new life, or life in covenant with God. The implied voice of *theopneustos* is present and passive: it is a living God who breathes newness of life into a people, in

this case through scriptural medium rather than creation's "dirt"/"ground" or the prophet's "fourfold spirit."

12. Scripture's fourfold usefulness that includes both its priestly (teaching, training) and prophetic (showing mistakes, correcting) roles is also patterned on how rabbis used scripture to guide observant Jews. Timothy imitates Paul the Pharisee who was trained to use scripture to reprove and correct false teachers while teaching and training a congregation to live holy lives before God and each other. Such are the aspirations and "good work" of "the man of God" (3:17a) who is brought to maturity by scripture. In fact, the repetition of "mature . . . make mature" (3:17) draws upon rarely used words from a glossary of spiritual formation that envisages a process during which things are added to make a person or group complete. In other words, scripture's different uses supply goods that add to whatever else has been received from the tradition—in this case, from observing Paul's life and listening to him teach (3:10–13).

13. The scope of the purpose clause ("so that," 3:17) of scripture is debated, whether it refers to a single "man of God" (= Timothy) or to the pastor's entire congregation. Most interpreters admit that even if referring only to Timothy, the formative role of scripture in producing "every good work" applies to all. This phrase, "every good work," is repeatedly used in the PE (in 1 Tim 2:10; 2 Tim 2:21; 3:17; Titus 1:16; 3:1; and similarly in 1 Tim 3:1; 5:10, 25; 6:18; Titus 2:7, 14; 3:8). The exemplary public life produced by God's saving grace is characterized in the PE by those cardinal virtues Paul often speaks of as evidence of the transforming effect of God's grace. This moral payoff is the target of the redeemed community's use of its every scripture.

14. Paul's use of the familiar theological formula "in the presence of God" (4:1) introduces the end-time result of a life well lived for God's sake (cf. 1 Tim 2:3; 5:4, 21; 6:13; 2 Tim 2:14). Its use here is extended by a call to action made more urgent by the return ("appearing") of the reigning Christ to complete his messianic work as "judge of the living and the dead" (cf. 1 Tim 5:21). This belief probably reaches back to 2:8–10 for clarification that his future judgment includes members of the community who have denied the faith (2:12–13). Timothy's future will also be measured by whether or not he has remained faithful to "the pattern of healthy teaching" that God entrusted to Paul (1:12–13; cf. 1 Tim 4:14–16).

15. The principal command given Timothy is to "proclaim (*kērussō*) the word (*logos*)" (4:2a; cf. 1:13; 2:15; 1 Tim 4:14–16). The four commands

he adds—"stand ready . . . refute . . . rebuke . . . encourage" (4:2b)—elaborate the purpose of this main one. The message Timothy is charged to proclaim follows the "pattern" of Pauline teaching (cf. 1:13; 2:8b–9). The normal sense of the verb "proclaim" is a public speech that clarifies truth. Timothy's proclamation imitates Paul in refuting falsehoods (4:3–4; cf. 3:1–9) to clarify the gospel (4:8). The connection of Paul's earlier affirmation of scripture's inspiration and usefulness underwrites its primary role in clarifying the truth about God, whether in preaching that teaches and trains or shows mistakes and corrects.

16. I have translated *mythoi* as "conspiracy theories" (4:4) to help create a more contemporary word-picture to target what scripture "corrects" (cf. 3:16). Conspiracies propose counternarratives of the truth—"fake news"—often found in those congregations that "turn away from the truth" because they do "not tolerate healthy teaching . . . and accumulate teachers who say what they want to hear" (4:3–4). I would argue that Paul's repeated warning of those "intolerant" of his gospel of salvation is "the most important normative concept in the PE."[1] The prophetic use of scripture to correct mistakes when teaching the truth of the gospel includes *how* to preach the message of salvation, not only what to preach. Good pedagogy and good theology are of a piece.

17. Paul's final *se de* ("you, however"; 4:5; cf. 3:10, 14) introduces another contrasting image of Timothy as his faithful successor. In contrast to those spreading conspiracies, he "remains sober-minded" (4:5). The sober-minded are those who press for continuity with the past—in this case, to maintain what is remembered of Paul. For this reason, this concluding exhortation is made more emphatic by Paul's deeply personal testimony: "as for me" (4:6) begins Paul's prediction of his imminent death (4:6), his assessment of a faithful life (4:7), and confidence in his reception of a "champion's wreath" when the Lord returns to judge the living and the dead (4:8; cf. 4:1). This reminiscence concludes in the genre of a letter of succession: a formal announcement of the leader's impending "death" (4:6, lit. "departure") that cues his succession so that his life's work continues beyond death (4:7–8).

18. Paul anticipates a "champion's wreath of righteousness that the Lord will give me on that day" (4:8a). The reason for his optimism is supplied by the memorable triad of verbal metaphors in the perfect tense to underscore these are his completed goals: "I have fought the fight, finished

---

1. Childs, *Church's Guide for Reading Paul*, 163.

the race, kept the faith" (4:7). He is not motivated by prospect of a "champion's wreath" but by his understanding of Christ whose faithfulness to God resulted in his exaltation as Lord (Phil 2:5–11). In this sense his two assertions that "I have kept the faith" and a "crown of righteousness is reserved for me" (4:8) are paired. This climactic pairing recalls his quotation of Hab 2:4 in Rom 1:17 to keynote the presentation of his proclaimed gospel (Rom 1:15): "the righteous shall live by faith."

Preaching 2 Timothy 3–4

Sermon big idea

The concluding passage from 2 Timothy concentrates us on what many consider the issue that occasioned the writing of Paul's second letter to Timothy: Paul's growing awareness of his death without witnessing Jesus's return, perhaps alluded to in other canonical letters (e.g., 1 Thess 4:15; Rom 11:11–32), prompts him to speak to Timothy of a final succession that would "fulfill your ministry" (4:6–8). As I have suggested in my exegetical notes, Paul's concluding exhortation enlists three indispensable elements of a believer's formation into a "person of God" (3:17) enabled by the inspiring Spirit to do God's work in a competent and compliant way. A three-point sermon, then, would develop each of these elements: (1) follow the exemplary leader (3:10–14), (2) use scripture (3:15—4:4), and (3) preach the gospel for today (4:5–8). While the audience could well be the preacher's entire congregation, the context of this passage may focus in a particular way on the congregation's spiritual leaders. Likewise in a classroom, teaching this passage may direct its careful instruction at those called into Christian ministry—a seminary classroom or any class that gathers those gifted few who sense a call to ministry.

Sermon sketch

The three points of this sermon follow naturally the flow of the passage ordered by Paul's repetition of the introductory and emphatic address "You, however." A sermon on this passage may also begin with such an address, whether of a congregation or a classroom. The "however" of this address presumes conflict or contrast between "people of God" (3:17) and those who promote falsehoods as "the truth." Messaging is important in our world.

This is a sermon about staying on message in the face of rival messages, whether secular or religious, and the growing distrust in the truthfulness of the Christian gospel. Clearly, Paul's threefold charge has in mind those practices that form the gifted and called messenger of this gospel: congregations of the one holy catholic and apostolic church.

1. *"You, however, have closely observed me"* (3:10). I doubt any of us have lived our lives without a role model to imitate. We see someone who looks like us doing or saying things we thought impossible for the likes of us and we are inspired to follow their lead. Leadership is mostly providing good examples for others to imitate. Whether parents, workers, students, or believers, we know the value of following the lead of exemplary others. Certainly Paul understands the importance of his life as the personification of the kind of faithfulness that he desires for Timothy, and for those whom Timothy leads. The first point can explore the different areas of influence that Paul mentions as they might apply to the congregants or students for whom clergy and faculty provides examples for them to imitate. The "however" of this opening exhortation (3:10) concerns those false teachers and disrupters Paul mentions in the PE who should not lead and should not be imitated by God's people.

2. *"You, however, stay steady in what you have learned and found convincing"* (3:14). While some Christian traditions emphasize the importance of learning God from a variety of sources (including our role models), Paul concentrates on the importance of using "every scripture" as the principal medium of God's word. This passage in perhaps the most important biblical text about the importance of biblical texts and should be handled with care and completeness. Paul's bold and expansive affirmation of scripture regards its "nature" as divinely inspired, its fourfold role—to teach and train and to show and correct mistakes—and its twofold purpose—to impart the wisdom needed for salvation and to form saints capable of every good work of God. The second "however" (3:14) suggests that a scripture-formed discipleship (3:15–17) objects to any practice of Christian formation that "will not tolerate healthy teaching" (4:3).

3. *"You, however, remain self-controlled . . . do the work of a preacher of the good news"* (4:5). The final "however" draws the reader's attention to Paul's farewell (4:6–8). On the one hand, a "sober-minded" Timothy is contrasted to those who are drawn to conspiracy theories (4:5); on the other hand, however, young Timothy is compared to an aging Paul whose ministry has been poured out as a holy libation to God (4:6) and who has

finished the race with his faith firm to receive the victor's wreath. This final "however" imagines Timothy's unfinished résumé and what is left for him to complete. The preacher or teacher can conclude this series on 2 Timothy by asking the congregation or classroom to imagine where they now are in comparison to the apostle's standard: the future hardship yet endured, the ministry yet fulfilled, the libation yet poured out in God's presence provides the motive to continue the race until finished.

TITUS

A Snapshot of Titus

Paul's brief letter to Titus was folded into scripture's Pauline letter collection with 1–2 Timothy, thereby presuming their common role in forming congregations whose public witness is patterned after Paul's apostolic legacy. Titus is also received as a letter of succession, occasioned by Paul's absence (1:5) and his subsequent delegation of Titus, his "loyal child" (1:4; cf. 1 Tim 1:2), to continue the mission they had shared together in Roman Asia and beyond (1:5; cf. 2 Cor 2:13; 7:6–7, 13–15; 8:6, 26–28, 34; 12:18). This continuity of perspective is evident by the catchwords shared by these three "Pastoral" letters (e.g., Savior, sound doctrine, godliness), by the literary genres they employ (e.g., letter form, theological summaries, leadership credentials, household codes, catalogues of vices and virtues, personal instructions), and by the sociology of a Roman household that orders the congregation's public life.

Focus should not be placed on these similarities, however, but rather on what distinctive contributions Titus makes to the Pauline collection as a whole. More subtly, these similarities are applied to very different social locations—the urban and urbane Ephesus of Timothy and the uncivilized Crete of Titus (cf. 1:12)—in a way that intimates that Paul's gospel does not change from place to place: God is Savior of all people in equal measure (so 1 Tim 2:3–6).

At the same time, the slight differences detected in Paul's instructions to Titus may indicate the dynamic adaptability of this same apostolic tradition to different social settings. For example, Titus's Cretan congregation is less organized and spiritually mature and so needs "to be put in order" (1:5). Additionally, Paul's exhortation to Timothy to avoid selecting new converts for leadership (1 Tim 3:6) is nowhere found in Titus, which may suggest his congregation is filled with recent converts from a population that was only recently penetrated by the gospel. An awareness of this ambivalence puts the reader on notice that Paul's canonical witness is adaptable to ever-changing social worlds, as different today as Ephesus is from Crete.

More substantively, Titus contains two sustained theological reflections on the "epiphany of Jesus Christ" (2:11–14; 3:4–7), so important that the church continues to read them publicly on Christmas Day. The final two chapters of this commentary will consider each in turn. Together they supply the interpretive key that concentrates Paul's canonical witness to God's promised salvation, which is realized because of Jesus Christ. In particular, their use of both "salvation" and "Savior" of both God and Jesus Christ refuses modern criticism's tendency to separate God's providential action from Jesus's messianic death and resurrection. Significantly, Paul's second Christological summary (3:4–7) includes his most important formula of the Spirit's work within the Pauline collection. This intimate connection of Christ with the Spirit in the work of God's salvation effectively inclines the entire Pauline witness toward a Trinitarian understanding that humanity's spiritual renewal is the result of God's grace alone (3:7).

The Messenger *Is* the Message

1:1 From Paul, a slave of God and an apostle of Jesus Christ, according to the faith of God's elect ones and a knowledge of truth that agrees with godliness, ² in hope of eternal life that God, who does not lie, promised before time began [3] and revealed God's word in due time through the preaching entrusted to me by the command of God our Savior. [4] To Titus, my true child according to a common faith: grace and peace from God the Father and Christ Jesus our Savior.

[5] The reason I left you in Crete was to put right what is lacking there and to appoint elders in every city. As I directed you, [6] appoint only those who are without fault—the husband of one wife with faithful children who cannot be accused of self-indulgence or rebelliousness—[7] for it is necessary that the supervisor be without fault as God's household-manager, not stubborn, not irritable, not a drunkard or a bully, not acquisitive. [8] Rather, he should befriend strangers, befriend what is good, modest, upright, devout, under control, [9] with a firm hold on the teaching of the faithful word, so that he may be able to exhort with healthy teaching while refuting those who speak against it.

[10] For indeed there are many who are rebellious, who are unreasonable and mislead, especially those from The Circumcision. [11] They must be silenced because they have shaken up entire households, teaching what should not be taught for dishonest profit. [12] One among them, a prophet of their own choosing, said, "Cretans are always liars, evil beasts, gluttons for laziness." [13] This testimony is true. So refute them firmly that they may grow a healthy faith [14] and not pay attention to Jewish legends or the demands of people who have turned from the truth. [15] All is clean to those who are clean, but to those who are defiled and without faith, their mind and conscience are defiled. [16] They profess to know God but their works deny God; they are detestable, disobedient, and disqualified for every good work.

2:1 You, however, speak in a manner consistent with healthy teaching. [2] Older men are to be prudent, mild-mannered, healthy in faith, loving, patient. [3] Likewise, the manners of older women are to be reverent, not slandering nor addicted to heavy drinking but teachers of virtue, [4] so that they may mentor young women in loving their husbands and children, [5] in modesty, purity, good homemakers, subject to their own husbands so that God's word may not be ridiculed. [6] Likewise, encourage young men to be modest [7] in every way. Put yourself forward as a role model of good works, and in your teaching be sound and serious, [8] a healthy word above criticism, so that the opponent may respect us, finding nothing bad to say. [9] Slaves should be subject to their own masters in everything, to do what is asked without talking back, [10] not skimming from the top but demonstrating a good faith in all things, so that in everything they may adorn the teaching about God our Savior.

Celebrating Christmas Always, Part 1: The Grace of God Has Appeared

[11] For the Grace of God has appeared—salvation for all people!—[12] training us to abstain from godlessness and immoral affections to live modest, upright, and godly lives right now, [13] while we wait for the blessed hope and glory of the great God and the appearing of our Savior, Jesus Christ, [14] who gave himself for us to rescue us from total lawlessness and to cleanse a special people for himself, zealous for good works.

Celebrating Christmas Always, Part 2: The Love of God Has Appeared

[15] Talk about these things. Encourage and refute with complete authority; let no one disregard you. 3:1 Remind them to be subject to rulers and authorities, obedient, prepared for every good work. [2] They should disrespect no one, but be peaceful, kind, showing complete civility toward everyone. [3] For we too were once foolish, disobedient, deceived, enslaved to desires and various pleasures, living in evil and envy, hateful and hating others. [4] But when the Goodness and Kindness of God our Savior appeared, [5] God saved us—not because we had done righteous works but because of God's mercy—through a washing of regeneration and renewal in the holy Spirit, [6] whom God fully poured out upon us abundantly through Jesus Christ our Savior; [7] so that, having been put right by God's grace, we become confident heirs of the

hope for eternal life. [8] This saying is a core belief. And I want you to insist on these things, so that those who have come to believe in God may give careful attention to good works, which are good and useful for people.

Final Instructions and Greetings

[9] Avoid foolish controversies, genealogies, disputes, and battles for the Torah; they are without profit and useless. [10] After two warnings, have nothing more to do with a divisive person, [11] knowing that someone like that is twisted—he sins and condemns himself. [12] When I send Artemus or Tychicus to you, do your best to come to me in Nicopolis, for I've decided to winter there. [13] Eagerly send Zenas the lawyer and Apollos on their way so that they may lack nothing. [14] Let our people learn to devote themselves to good works to meet necessary needs so not to be unproductive. [15] Everyone with me greets you; greet those who love us in the faith.

Grace be with all of you.

Chapter 9

THE MESSENGER *IS* THE MESSAGE

Exegetical Notes on Titus 1

1. WHILE PAUL'S GREETING of Titus 1 (1:1–4) recalls the similar greeting of Timothy, this letter foregoes his customary note of thanksgiving and moves directly to stipulate the reason Paul writes it: his decision to leave Titus in Crete is "to put to rights what is lacking there" (1:5a). And what is lacking most in Paul's mission in Crete are spiritual leaders ("elders") who are "without fault" and whose résumé of leading a family household predicts they will also be effective in managing the affairs of the household of God (1:5b–9). This initial charge repeats Paul's instructions to Timothy (see my comments on 1 Timothy 3 above). While, according to Acts, Paul's missionary pattern includes the routine of appointing elders to supervise the formation of new congregations, what is more curious, when compared to the instructions of 1 Timothy 3, is the priority given in Titus to finding elders to lead the Cretan congregations. The conjunction "you see" (*gar*, 1:10) would seem to introduce a passage that explains why the appointment of competent elders to bring order among these new believers has become necessary: not only is the Cretan culture notorious for allowing disorderly behavior, there is a threat posed by "the circumcision" (1:10–16) who pay more attention to "Jewish myths" (1:14) than to "healthy teaching" (2:1) necessary in forming a "healthy faith" (1:13).

2. The historical identity of "the circumcision" is indeterminate due to our lack of information. Within the canonical context, however, this group is mentioned in the Acts narrative of the gentile Pentecost (Acts 10:45;

11:2). Apparently, they were a protest movement among Jewish Jesus-followers who policed Paul/Peter's more liberal interpretation of the initiation of repentant but uncircumcised (i.e., non-proselytized) gentiles into the covenant-keeping community. Their argument presumably appeals to Torah's requirement of circumcision for membership in the covenant-keeping community according to Genesis 17, which disagrees with Peter's revelation of God's will disclosed first in a vision (cf. Acts 10:9–16) but finally comprehended by the Spirit's subsequent baptism of a repentant Cornelius and his household (10:44–48; 11:15–17). Significantly, according to Paul's account of the Jerusalem meeting that settled this disagreement in Gal 2:1–10, the uncircumcised Titus (Gal 2:3) is symbolic of God's approval of his "mission to the uncircumcised" (Gal 2:7) and so of Jerusalem's decision to initiate faithful gentiles into the covenant-keeping community on the basis of their faith in Christ alone.

If mention of this group to Titus is cued by the preacher's prior reading of Acts 10–11 and Galatians 2, several things might be assumed: Titus represents a population of uncircumcised gentiles whose fellowship with God's people is predicated by their faith in God's word preached by the apostle Paul. That is, this conservative opposition party disagrees with the stunning claims of Paul's Torah-free gospel announced during his mission to the gentiles (so 1:3; note that Paul responds to these controversies in Romans, which should be read as background to his criticisms here in Titus 1) and they secure their disagreements by appealing to Torah's teaching that repentant gentiles, such as Titus, must maintain Judaism's purity practices, such as circumcision as covenant-keeping. Paul's appointment of Titus, an uncircumcised Greek, to take lead of his Torah-free mission to the "many rebellious people" of Crete may have stirred these rough waters even more! In any case, their protest seems to be over a particular kind of ritualized purity, which they claim is a condition of entering into covenant relationship with God for eternal life as disclosed in scripture by a God "who does not lie" (cf. 1:2b).

3. Paul's colorful profile of these false teachers (1:10–16) follows the rhetoric of polemics used in antiquity to castigate opponents and should not be taken literally. Rather than spiritual leaders who are "without fault" (1:6), they are religious renegades who have denied the truth of God's word disclosed to Paul and brought near to Cretans by Titus. The particular list of vices used in Paul's profile of protest includes several words found only here in the NT. Simply put, he chooses vices that are the reverse of those virtues

just listed of Christian leaders (cf. 1:7–9a). These are teachers who forge chaos rather than order, who subvert the gospel's truth about God's all-inclusive
grace rather than champion it, and who bring mischief into Christian households rather than encouragement and edification. Rather than exemplifying
the purity they demand of others, they lead to make a "dishonest profit" for
themselves (see my commentary on 1 Tim 6:3–10).

Epimenides of Crete (ca. 650 BCE) is probably the unnamed author of
the quotation Paul cites in verse 12 to castigate Cretans as liars and cheats.
Paul agrees with the assessment voiced by their own public intellectuals.
In the ancient world, the verb "to Cretonize" was often used in reference
to duplicitous acts! It may seem curious to Cretan Jews (including his opponents) that Paul would refer to Epimenides as a "prophet"—a carrier of
the word of the Lord. Theodoret, bishop of Cyprus (ca. 430–57 CE), com-
mented that Paul here quotes a pagan poet of the Greeks with irony, claiming him as God's prophet for those Cretans "from The Circumcision" (i.e.,
Jews) in order to silence their teaching of "Jewish legends" (or lies) instead
of God's truth (v. 14).[1] However, according to the *Seder Olam Rabbah* 21,
the non-Jewish world has its own "prophets" who speak accurately "of their
own" and should be heeded by them. Paul would allow, as would other Jewish teachers of his day, that pagans have their own truth-tellers who observe
carefully and speak accurately of their own people. In this sense, Aristotle
says of Epimenides the Cretan that he is not a prophet because he forecasts
the future but because he brings the hidden to light (*Rhet.* 3.17.10). But
in fact the low regard for Cretan integrity in religious matters was widely
shared, in part because some islanders actually claimed with straight face
that they possessed the tomb of the immortal Zeus (Callimachus, *Hymn
to Zeus*, 8–9)! While Cretan Jews certainly would not have shared this fic-
tion with their pagan neighbors, Paul may be coloring them with the same
cultural brush if only for rhetorical effect in making his larger point: only
he possesses God's word for this moment (see 1:3): these teachers have sub-
stituted "Jewish legends" for his "healthy teaching" (1:9).

4. The plural "legends" is generally used negatively in the ancient
world, not only because they are fictions that some parade as true but
because they then would appeal to these "truths" to justify an unhealthy
lifestyle (Plato, *Leg.* 1.636; *Rep.* 2.376E–383C). Josephus reports that some
Jews of Crete were susceptible to superstition (*Ant.* 17.327). More likely,
this is Paul's phrase for certain speculative midrashim about OT characters,

---

1. Twomey, *The Pastoral Epistles through the Centuries*, 193.

which were used to authorize beliefs and practices that opposed and even subverted Paul's witness. Likewise, the addition of "demands of the people" probably refers to various codes of conduct, based upon these speculations, which stipulated what was "clean" or "defiled." If Jewish in cast, then probably certain foods and purity practices related to proper "table fellowship" between Jews and repentant gentiles are implied.

5. The logic of the familiar (but cryptic) phrase that things are "clean to those clean but defiled to those defiled" is similar to Paul's argument against the ascetics in 1 Tim 4:1–5 (see commentary). While it is true that God's kingdom is "not food and drink but righteousness and peace and joy in the holy Spirit" (Rom 14:17), it remains the case that God is the Creator of good things, so that material goods, such as food, or social institutions, such as marriage, may be gladly received. Thus, the preacher/teacher must be careful not to generalize the meaning of this saying ("clean to those clean but defiled to those defiled") uncritically what is clean or defiled to current cultural or intellectual/scientific topics under debate. This often occasions a world-denying censorship that Paul repudiates in 1 Tim 4:1–5 and in his other canonical letters (e.g., 1 Cor 8–10; Col 2).

6. Paul repeats an earlier exhortation to avoid those teachers whose "public appearance is godly but who resist God's power" (see 2 Tim 3:5) in his contention that the circumcision professes faith in God but the manner of their life reveals that what they actually believe about God is fraudulent. Finally, the ritual idiom of "clean/defile" also recalls the topology of hygiene/disease widely used by moral philosophers to describe the human condition (see 1 Tim 6:4–5; 2 Tim 2:17). The opponents have diseased (or "defiled") minds and consciences, so that Paul charges Titus to find elders who can restore these teachers to a "healthy faith" (1:13) by instruction of "healthy teaching" (1:9). And Titus himself, as a faithful apprentice of the Pauline apostolate, must exemplify this by public speech "consistent with healthy teaching" (2:1). The optimism that Paul places to the act of public instruction is shaped by his Jewish tradition but is also rooted in a religious epistemology that an apostolic account of truth will always win out since it is communicated in the company of God's Spirit (cf. 1 Cor 2–4). The making of this point requires that Paul's instruction includes 2:1. Contemporary readers must make their own judgments about where the instruction begins and ends; in this case, I take issue with the later scribes who added chapter and verse markers to the manuscripts

they had received to copy and pass on, as I believe their chapter division here disrupts Paul's train of thought.

7. While church order is maintained by challenging the personal integrity of those who subvert the Pauline apostolate and the erroneous substance of what they teach others—and nowhere in the PE is the polemic of doing so sharper than in this passage—there is a remarkable consistency in stipulating a redemptive endgame. Perhaps illustrative of the Lord's epiphany to "rescue us from lawlessness and cleanse a people for himself" (2:14), the refutation of "the circumcision" does not purpose their excommunication but a rescue operation that seeks to restore them to a "healthy faith" (1:13).

8. What follows in Titus 2:2–10 rehearses a household code of conduct similar to what is received in 1 Timothy 5 (see commentary). The missional point of Paul's adaptation of a typical Roman family household—the kind of family unit widely discussed by philosophers and teachers of the Roman world—is the same in both epistles. Namely, to help the leader, Titus in this case, reimagine congregational relationships as similar to a family's well-functioning household in his social world. The pivot-point of this unit of instruction is found in the purpose clause that concludes 2:5: "so that God's word may not be ridiculed (*blasphēmeō*)."

Preaching Titus 1

Sermon big idea

As is often the case in scripture's paraenetic literature, the concluding verse often gives expression to a sermon's big idea. This seems true of this passage whose various moving parts—the lists of personal characteristics, Paul's highly charged polemical rhetoric, his mention of the circumcision's protest movement and repeated use of a family's household as typological of congregational life—are brought to focus by 2:1's contrasting assertion: Christian practices and character "speaks" (*laleō*) what is "healthy" or right teaching. Although a difficult text to translate, Paul underscores the connection between moral practice and preaching the gospel's truth—a claim that the apostle routinely makes in his canonical letters but is rarely repeated from the pulpit. In fact, more frequently one hears a contrary claim that God cares for the sinner, not the sin. If this misreading of scripture is embodied in the lives of Jesus followers, one is bound to observe a kind of Christian fideism or "faith only" understanding of salvation that is conditioned on a profession of faith alone without a complement of good works that imitate Christ's righteousness and prove the genuineness of one's repentance.

Although it consists of bits and pieces and is difficult to fashion into a coherent sermon, this passage from Titus 1 offers the preacher an excellent opportunity to call the congregation to a way of life that embodies and testifies to the truth of God's gospel of grace.

Sermon sketch

The following three points may be made in unpacking this big idea for a congregation or classroom of students:

1. "There are many who are rebellious" (1:10a). The hard work of exegesis and theological interpretation involves the even harder work of contemporizing what the text says in a way that makes clear its relevance for today's audiences. Who are today's "rebellious people" within the church—those who have influence with other Christians but seem to mislead them away from God's word by promoting a gospel of prosperity or of cheapened grace; or perhaps a gospel that exchanges a political position or social posture for the gospel that focuses on the values of God's kingdom? Name them as Paul does here. Explain how they mislead believers. Make certain the names you choose and your descriptions of error are accurate.

2. "Refute them firmly that they may grow a healthy faith" (1:13b). Duplicating Paul's polemical rhetoric is very difficult to stage within any faith community. It easily leads to accusations of self-righteousness or taking sides and so dividing a congregation called to be one in Christ. Care must be taken in how the task of identifying those co-believers who nonetheless are "rebellious people" who subvert the faith. One way of creating an irenic atmosphere in order to do this prophetic work—something that may be easier to engage in a congregation or classroom where a high level of trust is found—is to emphasize the motive that Paul does in verse 13: the reason for correction is formative, not punitive. This work is not name-calling but redemptive of a people whose spiritual leaders hold firmly to the spiritual health of the faithful as their vocation. This point must be made clear and without equivocation. Correction, however controversial, must be made because the spiritual outcomes of a people are at risk by those who parade false ideas, positions, and practices—"fake news"—to others.

3. The messenger's character must be consistent with the message's content of what is truly true (2:1). The sermon's concluding point settles in on 2:1's climactic claim that we "speak" truth as messengers of God's redemptive word by living in a manner consistent with the truth of the gospel we proclaim for Christ's sake. A preacher should call into question any notion that we can separate out the manner of our lives lived and the gospel message we preach as the truth. Truth is lived. With the testimony of a life transformed by God's grace from vice to virtue the congregation puts into play the hard evidence the secures what they claim or teach as the gospel truth.

Chapter 10

CELEBRATING CHRISTMAS ALWAYS, PART 1: THE GRACE OF GOD HAS APPEARED

Exegetical Notes on Titus 2

1. THE OPENING OF Titus frame this initial summary of Paul's gospel. The apostle's initial charge to Titus is to appoint virtuous leaders of congregations planted across the island of Crete who will help him safeguard the faith of new believers against the threat of false teachers who profess to know God but whose deeds deny God (1:5–16). He then instructs Titus to cultivate the moral and spiritual order of these congregations (2:2–10a) that align with sound doctrine (2:1), so that in every social relationship the community "may adorn the teaching about God our Savior" (2:10b). Paul's grand pretext in providing these moral instructions to Titus is that the Christian life embodies the truth claims of the Christian gospel for all to see—a sight that is hardly repulsive but rather highly attractive to those who look on (2:5, 8, 10).

2. This passage is one of several theological summaries found in the PE. Most are attached to exhortations to Timothy and Titus about invigorating their own ministry of the gospel in continuity with Paul's and are carefully crafted to fit the immediate situation. In fact, our lesson begins with a connecting *gar* ("for," 2:11) to cue the reader that what follows explains what precedes it. Closer scrutiny shows that Paul has just concluded his instructions with a purpose statement: the positive aim of the community's

life together is to "adorn the teaching about God our Savior" (2:10b). The verb "adorn" (*kosmeo*) comes from the "cosmos/-ic" word family and among its most popular connotations is of a "cosmetic" change that one applies to make one's public appearance more appealing. According to Paul, healthy relationships between believers provide the external "cosmetic" that makes the inward beliefs and values of our faith more presentable to the world: believers should be the very picture of theological and spiritual health.

3. This crucial claim is made even clearer by repetition of key words that link together this purpose clause (2:10b) with the opening line of the theological summary (2:11): "in everything" is picked up again by "*all* people," and the very character of "God our *Savior*" is envisaged by the dramatic exclamatory "*salvation* for all people!" Pauline theology is missionary theology; it is never preoccupied with declining the nouns of God's existence but rather with conjugating the verbs of God's saving activity in the world. Sharply put, then, if the household code given in 2:2–10a is the moral "cosmetic" the church applies for the world to see, then 2:11–14 is the doctrinal statement of God's salvation that provides its theological explanation. As Jim Sanders frequently reminded his students, the effective preacher never moralizes without theologizing.

4. The uncommon language and rhetorical shape of this passage suggest that Paul may have used a preformed confession of faith known to Titus. It is written in a single Greek sentence that makes clearer that its various parts form a complete and coherent whole. Here, then, Paul reminds Titus of the two core beliefs that constitute the "doctrine of God our Savior." The first belief is that the grace of God has already appeared (lit. "epiphany") to bring salvation for all people (2:11). The unusual personification of grace is a poetic way of recalling the person of Jesus, whose appearance in human history is the subtext of this entire passage, as made clear by 2:14. Even so, Paul clearly wants Titus to reflect upon the community's actual experience of God's grace—grace alone, its meaning and singular importance for advancing the gospel.

5. This passage mentions two core beliefs about this experience of God's saving grace, both with implicit reference to the prior instructions for the household of faith (2:2–10a). The first belief that controls the theological grammar of Paul's gospel regards the sphere of God's grace, which Paul's gospel claims extends to all people. Although the reason to press for the inclusiveness of salvation is not made clear, he probably has the household code (rather than his opponents) in mind. That is, the grace of God is equally

shared by every member of the faith community: God excludes no one by gender, age, ethnicity, or social class from full salvation (cf. Gal 3:28). For this reason, every member and every relationship of the household of God must exemplify the results of God's grace in their life together.

6. Paul elaborates his belief about God's grace by claiming that God not only saves the repentant *from* sin and death but also redeems them from sin's captivity—a new exodus that liberates them to live in new ways according to a righteous God's high standards (cf. Rom 6:1–14). Grace not only forgives sin but transforms lives. It is a power from God already at work "in the present age," since God's grace has already appeared for us on the cross and its power already demonstrated to us in the empty tomb. The sharp contrast between vice ("godlessness and immoral affections") and virtue ("modest, upright, and godly") in 2:12 expresses Christian conversion in practical terms: their real experience of God's grace "trains" or shapes believers into a moral people of the kind described in 2:2–10a. Again, the personification of grace presumes a subtext: the effect of divine grace in Christian formation is mediated by the Spirit through word and sacrament. In particular, the verb "train" (*paideuō*) refers to the practices of educating children—in this case, new converts who must learn the gospel under the tutelage of gifted teachers, such as the older women who, Paul says, have a responsibility to mentor the young women of the congregation (2:3–5). What is evocative here is that the moral education of new converts that Paul proposes relies not so much on the educational credentials of the mentors—although clearly from 2 Tim 3:10–14 this also is important—but on the grace that appears and enables them to shape the lives of their students by their example and instruction.

7. The second core belief about God concerns the future appearance of the "glory of our great God," for which the community must await the coming "of our Savior, Jesus Christ" (2:13). The confusing syntax of this verse is reflected in its different modern translations. Does the phrase "the glory of our great God" refer to the first or second person of the Trinity? Any response to this question is complex and remains contested. In my reading, Paul's understanding of God's promise according to Israel's scripture is that God's glorious presence in a restored Israel is ultimately realized at Messiah's return to earth to complete his mission to deliver all things from sin and death. Although the text's grammar suggests (but does not demand) that both God and Savior refer to Jesus Christ, the theological claim it enshrines suggests that the statement refers to both persons, even though Paul does

not conceive of the Father's present grace or future glory as somehow independent of the Son's death and *parousia*: God our Savior and "our Savior, Jesus Christ" make up the divine team of world saviors.

8. To what does the "glory of the great God" (2:13) refer that has its epiphany at our Lord's return? For what "appearing" is the faith community waiting? To understand this is to explain what prompts the community's hope in an unrealized future, which surely is the principal motivation to live in transformed ways during the present age. The "glory of God" is a prophetic idiom of an exilic people (esp. found in Isaiah and Ezekiel) and refers to the power and splendor of God's character that finally "will fill the whole earth." While Paul's primary concern lies with the concrete demonstration of God's glory at the end of human history, the consummation of God's reign of grace is also linked with the appearing (or return) of Messiah on earth. God's grace has already made its appearance in the messianic mission of the Suffering Servant "for the salvation of all people." Yet, this salvation and its transforming results (2:11–12) are harbingers of God's restored *creation* in which the redeemed community will live forever (cf. Isa 66:18–23).

9. The subtext of this striking personification of God's grace (2:11–12) and glory (2:13) to fulfill God's promised salvation is, of course, Christological and is now stated with profound clarity in 2:14. The past arrival of the Savior's grace and the blessed hope of the future arrival of the Creator's glory are both predicated upon the Lord's atoning death. Christ volunteers himself, a sacrifice for sin, both to "redeem us from sin"—the sinners' new exodus out of "Egyptian" captivity to sin and death—and "to purify a people for himself"—the liberated Israel's Passover in preparation for their long journey to their future promised land.

10. With the final phrase of 2:14, "zealous for good works," we come to the key to the interplay between moral teaching and theological confession that is found repeatedly in Titus (2:7, 14; 3:8, 14) and in similar phrases throughout the PE (1 Tim 2:10; 3:1; 5:10, 25; 6:18; 2 Tim 3:17). Why must the congregation of believers live according to the standard Paul establishes in 2:2–10a? Because the grace of God, which has already appeared with the death of Jesus "for us," is the power of a transformed life, purified from sin to live a life of good deeds—a life that heralds the coming triumph of God over sin and death once for all. Indeed, Moses establishes the logic of covenant-keeping when he bids Israel to behave as

a "holy nation" by being "zealous for good works" in response to God's liberating grace (Exod 19:3–6).

Preaching Titus 2

Sermon big idea

The opening personification of God's grace gives preachers the sermon's big idea: "God's grace has appeared." Yet the aorist tense of its verbal idea locates the appearance of grace in the past, which provokes a tension this passage explores. The tension is that the passage also speaks of another, future appearance of divine grace. Grace is placed at the beginning and the ending of scripture's story of God's salvation—it is the appearing of grace that brings salvation to all people (2:11). But how does God's grace show up in the middle of this biblical story? Paul might respond that we locate it in a dialogue between these two appearances of the savior, past and future, that helps believers explain the tensions we experience in seeking to get free from "total lawlessness" (2:14) in order to live "the godly life right now" (2:12). We occupy the messy middle between these two appearances of the Savior in bringing salvation to all people. The proposed sermon would develop this bifocal idea of God's salvation-creating grace for a present world depicted by Paul as a slugfest between the godless and lawless and those "trained" by grace to do good, always from a perspective of the gains already in play from Messiah's past advent and in hope of what our great God promises will happen at his future advent.

Sermon sketch

Preaching a brief pericope of only four verses presents the opposite challenge to the preacher than preaching an entire chapter, offered by my commentaries on 1 and 2 Timothy. If preached during Christmas or the following season of Epiphany, then the preacher or teacher could contextualize what is proclaimed by locating it in a particular season and its central themes: the birth of the Messiah, celebrated at Christmas, might be the springboard for interpreting and communicating the significance of his first appearance. Likewise, any commentary on Epiphany and the season that follows concentrates on what is seen or not of God when appointed witnesses catch sight of the appearance of God's salvation when meeting Jesus. This passage and the next both summarize Pauline witness to the appearance of grace in the coming of Jesus and its moral and spiritual implications for the community of his disciples. Here are the textual fragments I would suggest preachers parse to develop this three-point sermon:

1. *"For the Grace of God has appeared—salvation for all people!—training us . . . godly lives right now"* (2:11–12). The idea of God's salvation-creating grace occupies the epicenter of Paul's gospel. The idea proposed by the opening line of this passage personifies grace as a "trainer" who appears among a people saved by grace to teach them to reject the "godless" ways of the "world" for the "godly" ways of God. This would be a great time for preachers or teachers to use personal examples of transformed lives.

2. *"While we wait for the blessed hope and glory of the great God and appearing of our Savior, Jesus Christ"* (2:13). But this text also allows the preacher/teacher to talk about the struggle to live into the godly ways of God. The tension created by Paul's discussion of a past and future appearance of God's grace creates the kind of "already but not yet" ambivalence that explains the moral failures believers continue to experience this side of Christ's reappearance to consummate the history of God's full salvation. Even as Christian wait during Advent for the Christmas celebration of the promised Messiah's birth already realized, so we continue our wait for what has also been promised but not yet fulfilled: the full measure of God's reign of grace realized on earth as it has in heaven. Sin happens still. Death is still a guarantee of life. Christians feel the struggle between giving into the sin they are trained to reject and the good they desire to do. We wait for the full and final resolution of these deeply human tensions as a holy end of God's way of salvation.

3. *"Jesus rescued us from total lawlessness and cleansed a people who are zealous for good works"* (2:14). The literary brackets that surround mention of "the blessed hope" that forges a community's wait for God's final victory over sin and death (so 2:13) are both expressions of grace at work to transform believers from bad news to good news: we are "trained" by grace to reject ungodliness for God's ways (2:12) and we are set free by Christ from lawlessness to become a people eager to do good (2:14). What I take as the crucial message of this text is that working out of God's saving grace offers more than a forgiveness of sin and a new identity as God's people (2:13). God's grace offers all people the real prospect of moral transformation.

Chapter 11

CELEBRATING CHRISTMAS ALWAYS, PART 2: THE LOVE OF GOD HAS APPEARED

Exegetical Notes on Titus 3

1. TITUS 3 EXTENDS the teaching of Titus 2 by supplying additional theological markers to secure Paul's exhortations to Titus, especially regarding his formation as a minister of the gospel and the life of his congregations in Crete. Readers will note that the Epistle to Titus uses a set of common themes and language to summarize Paul's account of God's purpose and plan of salvation. The dynamic interplay between Christian beliefs and Christian behavior, characteristic of the PE, follows and helps to interpret the deep logic of Paul's gospel: God's grace which forgives sinners also transforms believers to live in new ways that accord with God's plan and purpose for humans. Believers become "new creatures" (2 Cor 5:17).

2. This transformation of "convict into convert" is well illustrated by the sharp contrast Paul makes between the chapter's opening exhortation to be "good citizens" (3:1–2) and the catalogue of human vices that follow (3:3). The imperial cast of Paul's exhortation in 3:1–2 is not without controversy, since his appeal to do the bidding of those in charge seems to some to subvert the countercultural dimension of Christian community. Yet the sharp contrast between virtue and vice found throughout the canonical collection of Pauline letters illustrates well the theological point expressed in the confession of faith that "God is our Savior in everything" (2:10), whose

grace "appears" not only to "train" new believers (2:11–12) but first of all to transform sinners for new life of good works that are pleasing to God.

3. Titus 3:4–7 is the second Pauline confession of faith found in Titus (cf. 2:11–14) and includes perhaps the clearest summary of Paul's theology of the Spirit found in his canonical letters (see 3:5–6); the importance of this text, then, cannot be overstated. Articulated in a single sentence as another of the PE's "faithful sayings" (3:8a), this confession begins as did 2:11 with a personified epiphany: God "appeared" as Love and Kindness. The temporal phrase "But when" not only introduces a soft contrast with the vice list of 3:3 but recognizes that a decisive change of direction has already taken place in human history because God's grace has already made its appearance "through Jesus Christ our savior" (3:6; cf. 2:11) and at Pentecost "in the holy Spirit" (3:5; cf. 2 Tim 1:8–10). As a result, sin ends for the moral rogue depicted in 3:3, who becomes a good neighbor capable of loving others as encouraged in 3:2.

4. The two divine virtues Paul mentions in 3:4—"goodness" (*chrēstotēs*) and "kindness" (*philanthrōpia*)—characterize the God who first "appeared" to save humanity (3:4) and then to restore a redeemed humanity in the image of God to be good and act kindly toward others. The aorist indicative of the verbal idea locates "God our Savior's" appearance in humanity's past experiences of divine love and kindness because of Jesus Christ who is also called "our Savior" (3:6). The believers' experiences of God's grace are first of God's love and then of their own new ability to love and show kindness to one another (cf. 1 John 4:7–14), which are the marks of those "good works" that benefit all people (3:8).

5. What follows from God's epiphany as Love and Kindness is a richly textured confession of the grand evangelical affirmation that "God saved us" (3:5). Its rhetorical design is framed by another contrast, expanding upon the contrast just considered, between our failed attempts to earn God's salvation by "righteous works" (3:5a) and the victory of God "because of God's mercy" that is experienced by the "renewing of the holy Spirit" (3:5b). Of course, the contrast between human works and divine mercy—expressed in considerable rhetorical/lexical variety in the Pauline letters—is the pivot point of Paul's gospel to the non-Jews and so also for Titus's mission in Crete. In this instance, the conflict between human works and divine mercy is made even more emphatic in the Greek text by placing the main verbal idea, "God saved us," *after* the contrast is asserted (rather than before it, as in most translations). Often in Paul's letters the

phrase "because of works" is attached to doing the law as an ineffective means of acquiring God's saving grace.

6. In making this point, Paul is responding to a controversy (and its related theodicy) occasioned by his law-free gentile mission: everyone is a sinner, whether Jew or non-Jew, and in need of baptism into the faith community covenanted with God for salvation by trusting in the results of Jesus' messianic death alone. In this text the meaning of the phrase "righteous works" is much broader and intends to subvert *any* human activity, no matter how pleasing it may be to the righteous God of Israel. God's saving grace breaks into our lives because of Jesus, not because of our good deeds.

7. It is important to note that in both confessions received by Titus, Paul does not rule out "good works" as a divine imperative. The mark of those who truly belong to God is not set out as a public profession of faith according to these very confessions but rather by a repentant people's "eagerness to do good" (2:14) or their seriousness to perform "good works" (3:8). The faith community's "readiness for every good work" (3:1) is not only a matter of human agency—God does not perform good works on our behalf—the logic of Paul's gospel that true repentance produces the fruit of good works in keeping with it underwrites the opening transformation from what "we once were" (3:3) to a readiness for good work (cf. 3:1–2).

8. Confessions like this one are both compressed and severely gapped statements of a community's core beliefs. They provide glossaries of salvation-words that are imprecise if read as normative theological definitions. Some scholars suppose this passage, or something very similar to it, was used as part of an early Christian baptism liturgy when new converts were initiated into the congregation's life. In Titus, however, the purpose of this passage (along with 2:11–14) is rather more modest: to enlist those big catchwords to remind readers of Paul's theological legacy and its importance for the future of the church.

In particular, the passing reference to "in the holy Spirit" (3:5) is linked to the believer's "washing, regeneration, renewal"—a triad of catchwords that elsewhere in the Pauline collection refer to a community's spiritual formation. Although finding logical relationships or fine distinctions between these properties of the Spirit's work in transforming the believer's life is difficult, the grammar seems to commend pairing the words "regeneration and renewal" as the sum effect of the Spirit's "washing" (= baptism). "Regeneration" refers to the Spirit's work in mediating God's salvation-creating grace, whereby the believer experiences life in brand-new ways. "Renewal" is similar in meaning, although in Pauline thought the idea seems to be associated with transforming the way we think (Rom 12:2; Col 3:10), not only to know God's will but then to embody what we come to know as the truth in public places—as "living sacrifices" to God (Rom 12:1). In Acts, however, the Spirit's baptism (or "filling") is more "prophetic" and tied explicitly to the community's power to evangelize. The issue at stake for Paul is the believer's moral and spiritual transformation from a life of vice to one of virtue (cf. Gal 5:16–26). In this regard, the meaning of "regeneration and renewal" seems to envisage, however vaguely, a maturing process (cf. 2:11–12)—some even think in two distinctive ("regeneration" → "renewal") stages—by which the new believer becomes a morally competent person.

9. Significantly, this Spirit is "poured out" (*ekcheō*) upon the faith community "through Jesus Christ our Savior" (3:6). The idiom of the Lord pouring out the Spirit of prophecy recalls the Day of Pentecost when the Spirit is "poured out" (*ekcheō*) upon God's people (Acts 2:33) according to the *ekcheō* of biblical prophecy (see Acts 2:17–18). Paul extends the Spirit's work within the community beyond its initial Pentecostal outpouring to mediate God's transforming grace, especially noted in the good work of sharing possessions within one another (Acts 2:46–47). The collaboration of God and Christ in the Spirit's work of moral transformation is indicated by reference to "Jesus Christ our Savior" (3:6), which repeats the earlier "God our Savior" (3:4). The preposition "through" commends the messianic mission of Jesus, and especially his death (3:7), as the trigger event of the Spirit's arrival at Pentecost. That is, there could be no Spirit baptism, with its effective results of regeneration and renewal, without the birth, life, death, and resurrection of the Messiah.

It may be useful for the preacher to link this overarching idea of the Spirit with Paul's catalogue of the Spirit's "fruit" (Gal 5:22–26). The social virtues listed by Paul in Galatians include "kindness" and "love," which are also among the personifications of "God our Savior" mentioned in Titus 3:4. That is, Paul locates the Spirit's agency in the outworking of God's salvation in the social or moral formation of a community in which the Spirit dwells. A theological formula that depicts the arrival of God's salvation with "Jesus Christ our Savior" in terms of the Spirit's regenerating work is the centerpiece of Paul's reformulation of our understanding of the Spirit's agency in the economy of God's salvation.

10. Not only our present life with God in the holy Spirit, but any idea of a future with God—any hope of becoming "heirs of eternal life" (3:7)—would be rendered moot without Christ. In fact, 3:7 states the ultimate purpose ("so that," *hina*) of God's collaboration with Jesus Christ in our final justification: sinners are "put right" (*dikaioō*) by God's grace in order to live with God forever. Paul does not mean by eternal life "a slice of pie in the sky when we die." His hope of eternal life presumes a quality (not quantity) of real-life existence in a right relationship with God and each other that realizes the Creator's very good intentions for human creation. In this sense, to be "put right" is to be remade into those persons intent on doing the "good works" of God (3:8).

Preaching Titus 3

Sermon big idea

My suggestion is to preach or teach this passage with Titus 2:11–14; we receive them as an interpenetrating pair of important summaries of Paul's theological grammar. For a pastor or professor interested in catechizing their congregation or class into a deeper understanding of Paul's witness to God's salvation, this pair of passages from Titus is a good place to start. Titus 3 provides a congregation or class with a set of evocative images that will ground a good introduction to Paul's distinctive and radical idea of God's Spirit.

Sermon sketch

If this is a three-point sermon whose purpose is to teach people about Paul's witness to God's Spirit, here are the three texts I would work on, always with recall of and interaction with work previously done with Titus 2:

1. *"When the Goodness and Kindness of God our Savior appeared, God saved us"* (3:4–5a). If the sermon's big idea is introduced with a question—what do you believe about the holy Spirit?—and here preachers may even invite the congregation to give answers or a teacher could begin class with a discussion of this question—connection could be made with the "fruit of the Spirit" passage in Galatians 5. The idea of "spiritual fruit" should be familiar to most. Paul's list of Spirit fruit begins—and many scholars think is concentrated by—the first mentioned, "kindness," while

"goodness" is placed at the very center of Paul's list. God "appears" and is made "evident" (Gal 5:22) by the byproduct of the Spirit's work in cultivating a community's loving relationships (cf. 1 Tim 1:5).

2. *God saved us through the washing of new birth and renewing of the holy Spirit whom God fully poured out on us through Jesus Christ our Savior* (3:5b–6). The second point scored by this sermon works with two key Pauline catchphrases of the Spirit's regenerating or "renewing" work in transforming believers from bad news into good news by grace through faith. The preacher might take time to define and illustrate these phrases that sum up Christ's agency in the Spirit's work of full salvation—"washing of new birth" and "poured out on us." (See exegetical notes.)

3. *"So that having been put right by God's grace, we become the confident heirs of eternal life"* (3:7). Not only is the Spirit's work mediated through the agency of the risen Christ but it also heralds the consummation of God's salvation and the community's expectation of eternal life. It is important, however, not to detach this final point about eternal life from a transformation of present existence of those who place their confidence in God and are intent on performing good works (3:8). Paul's idea of the Spirit's work in the economy of God's salvation does not stop with God putting right a forgiven sinner's relationship with God; it includes the transformation of a faithful community's relationship with the world in which it is ready and willing to engage in "every good work" as good citizens for all people (3:1, 8).

BIBLIOGRAPHY

A Selection of Preacher-Friendly Commentaries on the Pastoral Epistles[1]

Bassler, Jouette M. *1 Timothy, 2 Timothy, Titus*. ANTC. Nashville: Abingdon, 1996.

Calvin, John. *The Second Epistle of Paul the Apostle to the Corinthians and the Epistles to Timothy, Titus and Philemon*. Grand Rapids: Eerdmans, 1964.

Chrysostom, St. John. *The Homilies of St. John Chrysostom, Archbishop of Constantinople, on the Epistles of St. Paul the Apostle to Timothy, Titus, and Philemon*. Translated by J. Tweedy. Oxford: Rivington, 1853.

Collins, Raymond F. *1 & 2 Timothy and Titus: A Commentary*. NTL. Louisville, KY: Westminster John Knox, 2002.

Fee, Gordon D. *1 and 2 Timothy, Titus*. NIBC. Peabody, MA: Hendrickson, 1988.

Hutson, Christopher R. *First and Second Timothy and Titus*. Paideia. Grand Rapids: Baker Academic, 2019.

Johnson, Luke T. *The First and Second Letters to Timothy*. New Haven, CT: Yale University Press, 2001.

Kelly, J. N. D. *A Commentary on the Pastoral Epistles*. BNTC. London: A. & C. Black, 1963.

Marshall, I. Howard. *The Pastoral Epistles*. ICC. Edinburgh: T. & T. Clark, 1999.

Mounce, William D. *The Pastoral Epistles*. WBC. Nashville: Nelson, 2010.

Ngewa, Samuel. *1 & 2 Timothy and Titus*. ABC. Grand Rapids: Zondervan, 2009.

Padilla, Osvaldo. *The Pastoral Epistles*. TNTC. Downers Grove, IL: InterVarsity, 2022.

Robinson, Anthony B., and Robert W. Wall. *Called to Lead: Paul's Letters to Timothy for a New Day*. Grand Rapids: Eerdmans, 2012.

Towner, Philip H. *1–2 Timothy and Titus*. Downers Grove, IL: InterVarsity, 1994.

Twomey, Jay. *The Pastoral Epistles through the Centuries*. Oxford: Wiley-Blackwell, 2009.

Wall, Robert W. *1 & 2 Timothy and Titus*. THNTC. Grand Rapids: Eerdmans, 2012.

1. The most comprehensive bibliography on the Pastoral Epistles available to either preacher or teacher is compiled and annotated by Chuck Bumgardner and found online at his blogsite: https://pastoralepistles.com/author/chuckbumgardner/.

Other Sources Cited

Campbell, Douglas A. *Pauline Dogmatics*. Grand Rapids: Eerdmans, 2020.

Childs, Brevard S. *The Church's Guide for Reading Paul: The Canonical Shaping of the Pauline Corpus*. Grand Rapids: Eerdmans, 2008.

Fretheim, Terrence. "Genesis." *New Interpreters Bible*. Vol. 1. Nashville: Abingdon, 1994.

Glahn, Sandra. *Nobody's Mother: Artemis of the Ephesians in Antiquity and the New Testament*. Downers Grove, IL: InterVarsity, 2023.

Hoag, Greg. *Wealth in Ancient Ephesus and the First Letter to Timothy*. BBRSup. Winona Lake, IN: Eisenbrauns, 2015.

Levenson, Jon. "Genesis." In *The Jewish Study Bible*, edited by A. Berlin and M. Z. Brettler. London: Oxford University Press, 2004.

Lincoln, Andrew. *Ephesians*. WBC. Dallas: Word, 1990.

Payne, Leah. *Gender and Pentecostal Revivalism*. London: Palgrave Macmillan, 2015.

Taylor, Charles. *A Secular Age*. Cambridge: Harvard University Press, 2007.

Trobish, David. *Paul's Letter Collection: Tracing the Origins*. Springfield, MO: Quiet Waters, 2009.